A Practical Guide To Kingdom Living: Unlocking Everyday Encounters
Sarah Crockett, beENCOUNTERed LLC
© Copyright 2019
www.beENCOUNTERed.com

Cover Design: Sarah Crockett
Editors: Lindsi Gross, Mary Crockett
Keyhole Image: www.freepngimg.com

ISBN: 978-0-578-58919-0

Notation for the translation of all Scripture quotations is listed next to the reference throughout the text.

Note: The author uses special capitalization when referring to Father God, Jesus, and Holy Spirit.

TABLE OF CONTENTS

Forward
Introduction

FORWARD

Sarah Crockett has never ceased to impress me since the very first day I met her. I was working on writing the curriculum for a course I was developing called *ACTIVATE* when a young woman I didn't know approached me. The first thing she said was "I want to assist you in whatever you are doing!" I politely said, "Sure, that would be nice" as one often says to politely divert an individual to avoid further interaction. However, as I turned to go on my way, the Holy Spirit said, "Don't discount this one so easily!" That coupled with her obvious sincerity and purity of intention made me reconsider. We exchanged contact information and the rest is, as they say, history. It was one of the best decisions I've ever made, just as deciding to read this book will be one of yours!

The humility Sarah walks in highlights the depth and width of her walk with the Lord! As you read A Practical Guide to Kingdom Living: Unlocking Everyday Encounters, you will see what I have been privileged to experience for some time now, a young woman full of wisdom and insight that could only come from long hours spent in God's Presence!

This book is titled well. It is, indeed, a practical guide to developing a supernatural lifestyle while growing in a personal relationship with God. It is a must read!

Papa Jim Evans, Director
Bethel Austin Transformation Center
Bethel Church Austin

Author of *ACTIVATE* and From the Panthers to The Pulpit.

INTRODUCTION

Welcome to NOW! This is one of my favorite sayings when it comes to encountering God's presence. Why? ...because one moment in His presence can change everything! In 2 Corinthians 3:18 (TPT) Paul explains, "We can all draw close to Him with the veil removed from our faces. And with no veil we all become like mirrors who brightly reflect the glory of the Lord Jesus. We are being transfigured into His very image as we move from one brighter level of glory to another. And this glorious transfiguration comes from the Lord, who is the Spirit." Every moment in His presence is a new now and has the potential to usher in another revelation or depth of intimacy with Him.

I was sitting in a pub in the west of England spending time with the Lord, having just met with a friend of friend that used to be the CEO of a publishing company, when the Lord began downloading the outline for this book. I share this to say that never in my life have I ever desired or imagined writing a book, let alone multiple books. My purpose in writing this book, is not only to be obedient, but also because I am passionate about equipping and activating others to know and release God's presence to the world. If sharing my testimonies and revelations can help you grow in intimacy and awareness in your relationship with God, then I say, "YES, Lord!"

Another reason I want to share testimony and revelation in this book comes from two promises found in the Word of God. First, revelation 19:10 (TPT) says, "...the testimony of Jesus is the spirit of prophecy." This verse promises that as testimonies are shared they will prophecy to the listener. Prophecy encourages, comforts, and builds us up. Standing on this promise I *know* that my testimonies will bring encouragement, comfort, and strength to your life! Why wouldn't I freely share?! The second promise is found in Revelation 12:11 (NKJV), "And they overcame him by the blood of the Lamb and by the word of their testimony..." Here we are promised that as we hear testimonies, we will overcome. I am confident, believing in His promise, that as you journey through each of these pages you will overcome in areas of your life where you have been struggling! Ephesians 6:17 tells us that the Word of God is the sword of the Spirit, and it is being wielded on your behalf!

I have great expectations for what the Lord is going to do in your life. My prayer as you read through this book, is that you will be taken from glory to glory as you encounter God's presence in new ways!

HOW TO READ THIS BOOK

Each chapter has an introduction to the topic, testimonies, teaching, and activations. The testimonies are intended to invite you into my process and journey and bring encouragement, comfort, strength, and overcoming (Revelation 19:10 and Revelation 12:11). Each testimony is also intended to build faith as we are promised in Romans 10:17 (NIV) that "faith comes from hearing."

The teaching in each chapter focuses on that chapter's topic. My teaching philosophy is to explain the why behind each subject and sharing the connection to the Word of God. I believe a balanced Christian life is rooted deeply in the Word of God and includes encountering God through spending time in His presence.

Each chapter ends with encounter activations. These are simple exercises for you to do to help you grow in your awareness and intimacy in encountering God's presence. I encourage you to approach each activation with an open heart. Some may push you outside of your comfort zone and that is the point. Peter didn't walk on water until he got out of the boat. The leper wasn't healed until he dipped in the river seven times. The 5,000 weren't fed until the boy offered up his lunch. Often the "more" of God is found in getting outside of our comfort zone.

THE GODHEAD

When I was first saved I did not understand relationship between Father God, Jesus, and the Holy Spirit within the Godhead and would attribute everything to God. This is true, They are all God, but I had yet to understand the distinction of each member of the Godhead.

Throughout this book I will refer to Father God, Jesus, Holy Spirit, God, Him, and Them. The purpose is threefold. First, I want to tell each testimony as accurately as possible. The testimonies you will read span many years and reflect different seasons and levels of revelation. Second, I want to encourage you to engage with the entire Godhead. When I had the revelation that I could interact with Father God, Jesus, and Holy Spirit I tapped into deeper depths of relationship and intimacy. I want that for you too! Finally, our relationship with Father God is shaped by our relationship with our earthly fathers, with Jesus by our siblings and friends, and Holy Spirit by our relationship with our mothers. If these relationships were strained in anyway it can affect how we relate to the Godhead. For example, it may be easier for you to connect with and hear from Jesus than Father God based on your experiences in childhood. Fear not, He can heal our wounds and the second section of the book is designed to bring freedom to any of these areas.

MY PRAYER FOR YOU
    I declare that you would have ears to hear, eyes to see, and a heart and mind that are open to His prompting and leading like never before. May you also experience immeasurably more than you have asked and imagined (Ephesians 3:20 NIV)!

SECTION I

CHAPTER 1
UNLOCKING KINGDOM LIVING

The key to unlocking an abundant life in the Kingdom of God is *relationship* built through communication. We must believe that God is speaking to us and follow through with obedience to His leading. Communication is the foundation to any relationship and our relationship with the Lord isn't any different.

In the Christian world communicating with God is what we call prayer. What comes to mind when you think about prayer? Does it bring excitement? Does it overwhelm you? Is it fun and easy or hard and laborious? Do you find yourself longing for more time to pray, always putting it off, or even avoiding it completely? Do you feel like your prayers are "powerful and effective" (James 5:16 NIV)? Regardless of how you view prayer, I want to invite you to approach this book by focusing on going deeper in your relationship with Father God, Jesus, and Holy Spirit.

The key to unlocking Kingdom Living is relationship. It's really that simple. It may feel complicated, but it really isn't. I promise. I often get asked what ministry school I attended or what type of training I received, and my answer is always that I learned on my face. I spent hours in the Word of God and the presence of God "sniffing" the carpet. Funny, but true. We are promised in   1 John 2:27 (NIV), "As for you, the anointing you received from him remains in you, and you do not need anyone to teach you. But as his anointing teaches you about all things and as that anointing is real, not counterfeit—just as it has taught you, remain in Him". No, I'm not opposed to learning from great teachers – I have. No, I'm not against ministry school – I attended one 10 years after getting saved. Yes, I believe in the local church and being under a covering. All I'm saying is that the Holy Spirit is a REALLY good Teacher and that I've learned so much from Him over the years. I'm also saying I like to learn directly from the Author and Teacher and not just from anointed, godly men and women.   Hear my heart. Accept the invitation before you to be taught by Holy Spirit as you spend time encountering His presence in relationship. He is our Counselor and Guide!

TESTIMONIES
Holy Interruption

I was driving across town for work and I immediately sensed that I needed to text one of my friends. There was no reason I should be thinking about my friend at that moment. It was the middle of the work day and my mind was on other things. When someone or something comes to mind so "randomly" I've learned to tune in and listen to what Holy Spirit is saying. As I took a moment to listen, I heard the phrase "I appreciate you." Simple, seemingly not profound. I appreciate anyone I call a friend, but I've learned to obey His nudge. This specific nudge felt urgent, so I immediately texted those three words to my friend. Later that afternoon I received a text back with cry face emojis and "you have no idea."

The truth is I don't need to know the who, what, when, where, or why of what was going on in her life at that moment. What I do know is that Holy Spirit knows all things, and He knew what my friend needed to hear in that exact moment. I'm thankful that I've cultivated our relationship enough that I am aware of both urgent and subtle nudges from Him. We're friends and friends have access to my life. I'm glad He spoke to me that day and I was able to be a part of encouraging my friend. It's what it means to partner with His presence.

Forgiveness and Healing

I am a part of the Prayer Ministry at my church and at the end of each service I have the privilege of praying for people. Recently a young woman came up for prayer with crutches and an ankle brace. Even though it might be obvious what someone wants prayer for, we always ask. I asked her and she confirmed she would like prayer for her ankle. I asked permission to touch her foot and began commanding the pain to leave. After a few seconds I asked her to test her foot and see if the pain level had changed or not. She reported that there was no change. I prayed again and commanded the pain to leave. She tested it again with no change. As a friend of

God, I know I'm not up there praying for people by myself. As I continued to lay my hand on her foot, I just asked Holy Spirit what to do. I immediately heard Him say to ask her if there is anything else she would like prayer for. I asked and with tears in her eyes she said, "regret." I didn't need her to go into details because I know when we have regrets we blame ourselves. I asked her if she would like to forgive herself and she said yes. I led her through a short repeat-after-me prayer into forgiving herself for whatever decisions were causing her so much pain and guilt. Then I asked if I could pray for her foot again. I asked Holy Spirit again how to pray for her foot and He showed me to release love as I held onto her foot. I spent a minute or so meditating on His love for her and asked her to test it again. This time she reported that she was feeling heat on her foot and the pain had been cut in half. Thank you Jesus! Remember, we always want to celebrate what He IS doing instead of focusing on what isn't happening! I laid my hand on her foot again and mediated on His love for her. When she tested it again the pain was GONE!!!

I'm so thankful that I am a friend of God. It was through my relationship with Him that I was able to help this young woman. I did what I had been taught to do, command the pain to leave, but through relationship I was able to ask what to do when that didn't work. He directed me in what to do bringing breakthrough and healing. He is so good!!!

God's Presence at Work

I arrived at a local school board building for a training session I was helping lead. I had never been to this building before, and when I walked in the door there was a woman speaking to the receptionist behind the desk. I asked where the training was being held and the woman in front of the desk offered to show me to the meeting room. As soon as she turned and spoke to me, I immediately felt the presence of God radiating from her countenance. We will discuss this in more detail later on in the book, but God can speak to us in many ways and in this moment He was giving me information. As she came to escort me to the meeting room I shared that I sensed the presence of God all over her. Remember, Peter didn't walk on water until he stepped out of the boat. When I mentioned what I was sensing I immediately began to hear more. I saw a picture of her praying and asked if she spent a lot of time in prayer. At this point, about twenty steps into the building, she was already in tears. She confirmed that she did in fact spend a lot of time in prayer. Next, I felt Holy Spirit nudge me to tell her that her prayers were powerful and effective. I shared what I was sensing and through her tears she said, "Who are you? I really needed this today." She thanked me and I walked into my meeting. The entire encounter probably lasted less than 2 minutes.

Who am I? I am a friend of God. I am the daughter of the King. I have a relationship with Him and I spend time in His presence getting to know who He is, who I am in Him, and His heart towards me. It's the time I spend in our secret place cultivating our relationship that allows for moments like these. Like a good friend or a spouse who you can glance at and have a ten-minute conversation without even speaking a word – this is what is possible for us as sons and daughters and friends of God!

The Checkout Line

Anyone who has a cat knows what it's like to stretch the litter a little too far. Maybe it's just me, but this was the current situation. I had gone to the grocery store several times with cat litter on my list only to find they'd run out of the type I wanted or I had forgotten to buy it completely. Late one evening when I realized something needed to be done, I hopped in the car to make a special trip just for cat litter. Why am I including all these details? ...because God can show up in the most practical of matters!

I grabbed the litter and headed to the checkout line. I waited for the few customers ahead of me to be served. While I was waiting I glanced over at my cashier and I immediately sensed the presence of God's radiating from her. It wasn't a physical sensation that I felt and it was also rather subtle, but when you know Him you recognize Him. After a few minutes it was my turn. I looked at her nametag and struck up the conversation and shared that when I first saw her I felt the presence of God. At this point I had nothing else. All I knew was that I felt God's presence coming from this woman. As I shared that, I immediately knew that she was needing some type of change in her housing situation. Again, we never want to add to or take away from what we are hearing, so I shared with her exactly what I sensed about desiring some type of transition with her housing situation. She responded rather shockingly and shared that she had just been talking to her daughter about that very subject the day before. I encouraged her that God knew her and her situation and wanted to let her know she is loved.

I needed cat litter. This woman needed to hear that God was aware of her situation. As we cultivate our friendship with God we begin to know Him more intimately and can more easily recognize when and what He is speaking to us.

Celebrating the Risk

I was working a table for my job at a large Christian concert that lasted all day long. Standing at a table all day can get rather boring so I decided that I would ask Holy Spirit how I could pray for people as they visited our table. After all, we were at a Christian concert. I started praying and asking people what they needed prayer for. If they didn't have any requests, I would just ask Holy Spirit what He wanted to say.

There were a lot of amazing testimonies from this experience, but there was one encounter with a young boy that stands out. This young boy came up to the table with his mother following just behind him. He began perusing our books and wondered if he could purchase one. I explained that they were not for sale and asked him if there was anything I could pray for him. He looked at me sort of puzzled and softly said no. I asked Holy Spirit what He wanted me to say and I sensed that this young boy was an artist. I asked if he was and he told me that he wasn't. I thanked him for stopping by and continued praying for others.

Why do I share this testimony? ...because we don't always

hear correctly. I had a choice to make when I missed hearing His heart for this boy. I could get discouraged and stop praying for people or I could celebrate the risk and keep trying. When Peter stepped out of the boat he walked on water...and then he sank into the waves. We don't focus on Peter's sinking, we celebrate his walking on water. Why don't we extend the same grace to ourselves? We should! It's the only way we will grow.

THINKING VS. LISTENING

As I mentioned before, communication is an integral part of relationships. I want to take a minute and address a very important part of our relationship with Father God, Jesus, and Holy Spirit. Communication is only possible with two parties involved, the sender and the receiver. The sender of a message does the talking and the receiver of the message can do one of two things - think or listen. The difference between thinking and listening is that when the receiver is thinking they are coming up with information based on their own understanding, and when they are listening they are getting information from the sender. Why does this matter in our relationship with God? When we ask Him a question looking for direction or an answer and the answer we get is formulated from what we *think* He would say, we aren't really giving Him a chance to speak into our lives. Ouch, huh?

If you only take one thing from this entire book, my prayer would be that you make space in your relationship with Father God, Jesus, and Holy Spirit to listen to what they want to speak over you, share with you, and reveal to you. This is a game changer! Again, many have asked over the years how I learned to cultivate His presence in my life. The answer is spending time in relationship, getting to know Him by asking questions, and taking the time to listen for His answers. Jesus paid for all believers to have this same access. It's available for you, too! I encourage you to ask lots of questions – fun questions, hard questions, directional questions, relational questions – He can handle it. He knows our hearts anyway, but when we invite Him into our process...that's when relationship happens. God is a relational God and even though He already knows, He wants to hear it from you!

ACTIVATION 1 – LISTENING
Instructions
Choose one scripture that is being highlighted to you. Write down a question you have about this scripture and spend some time listening for His answer to your question. Record what you hear.

What verse did you choose?

_____

What was your question?

_____
_____
_____
_____
_____

What revelation did you receive?

_____
_____
_____
_____

Takeaways from this Activation:

_____
_____
_____
_____
_____
_____

ACTIVATION 2 - BLESSING
Instructions

Ask Holy Spirit who He would like to encourage right now in this moment. Record the first name that pops into your mind in the space provided below. Now ask Holy Spirit what He wants to say to this person right now in this moment. (Note: This should always be encouraging and edifying. If you hear something negative release the opposite. For example, if you hear that they are in bondage, release freedom over them without mentioning bondage). Contact the person via text, email, or a phone call. Share what you sensed, no more and no less. It's important to always say what Holy Spirit is saying and not add to or take away from it. Then ask for feedback. Example questions to ask when gathering feedback include, "Does this mean anything to you?" or "Does this resonate?" If it does resonate with them celebrate and thank Jesus. If it does not, thank them for listening and bless them. Record your interaction.

Person's Name:

_____

What did you sense from Holy Spirit?

_____

_____

_____

_____

_____

Describe your interaction:

_____

_____

_____

_____

_____

_____

Takeaways from this Activation:

_____

_____

_____

_____

_____

ACTIVATION 3 – TAKING RISK
Instructions

When you are out and about (school, work, grocery store, bank, etc.) ask Holy Spirit to highlight someone. For example, at a bank it might be the bank teller you get, at the grocery store it might be your cashier, at work it might the custodian that cleans your office or the receptionist. It is not important that you know who the person is, remember God is not constrained by time or space. Once someone is highlighted, then ask the Holy Spirit what He wants to say to that person. You can ask for a short phrase, a scripture verse, a picture, or ask how He feels about them. The point is tuning into His heart for this person. Write down what you sense and share it with this person. Reflect on this experience after you have completed the activation assignment. Remember, celebrate the risk you are taking not the results!

Location:

_____

Who was highlighted?

_____

What did you sense from Holy Spirit for this person?

_____

_____

_____

_____

_____

Describe Your Experience:

_____
_____
_____
_____
_____
_____
_____
_____
_____

Takeaways from this Activation:

_____
_____
_____
_____
_____
_____
_____
_____
_____
_____
_____
_____
_____
_____
_____
_____
_____
_____
_____
_____

CHAPTER 2

EVERYDAY ENCOUNTERS

I was having encounters for several years before I learned there was terminology and language to describe what I was experiencing. I would simply tell others that I spent time hanging out with God or doing my quiet time. I believe many of you are having supernatural encounters in God's presence and you just don't have language for it. It's not your fault, we don't know things until we know things. Give yourself grace. We don't get mad at toddlers that don't know how to use a fork or teenagers when they are learning how to drive. If you don't know that's ok, but now that you realize that you don't know, you have the opportunity to grow. Why is it so hard for us to give ourselves grace when we are learning something? It's love that casts out fear, not punishment. Choose right now to give yourself grace when it comes to growing in your spiritual life. Trust me now, believe me later.

Now that we settled that, what exactly do I mean by encounter? An encounter is simply an experience that you have with Father God, Jesus, or Holy Spirit that brings transformation to your life. Transformation can come in many different "sizes". Often, transformation is viewed as something major, a billboard moment, or something huge. This is true, but not entirely. Just like the Israelites transformed the landscape of the Promise Land as they conquered it little by little (Exodus 23:29-31 NIV), we can experience transformation little by little as we have encounters in His presence. I'm not saying that the Lord can't majorly transform our lives in one moment; He definitely can. I am saying that sometimes He chooses to take us through a process in order to strengthen and secure us in Him.

Transformation can also come in many different "shapes". For example, a bible verse you read might leap off the pages and touch you deeply. You may have a worship song that you play on repeat that ministers to a situation or circumstance that you are going through. The Lord might use someone to give you a prophetic word, praying for healing, or to encourage you in an area that they did not know you were pondering or struggling with. Encounters can come from being directly in God's presence or He may choose to speak through a person. Colossians1:16 (TPT) reminds us that,

"For through the Son everything was created, both in the heavenly realm and on the earth, all that is seen and all that is unseen. Every seat of power, realm of government, principality, and authority—it was all created through Him and for His purpose." All things were created for His purpose! He even used a speaking donkey to encounter Balaam (Numbers 22:28-32 TPT) and confront his behavior.

The Lord is always with us (Matthew 28:20 NIV) and He is always speaking. Jesus purchased us access to approach His throne in freedom and confidence (Ephesians 3:12 NIV) anytime and anywhere we'd like. Encounters are available to us every day, all day. We simply have to learn to become aware of His presence in and around our lives! Let me share some of my testimonies to show you how simple and practical encountering His presence is in everyday things, like making grocery lists and buying birthday presents.

TESTIMONIES
Grocery List

One morning I was making a grocery list of items to pick up while I was out in the world that day. My friend was coming over for dinner and I needed few things to make the meal. As I wrote down the list, along with a few items I needed personally, I heard Holy Spirit interrupt and say, "Make banana bread for dessert". I was aware of His nudge; however, I was in the middle of trying to get out the door and on to work. As I was packing my bag, I heard Him again "make banana bread for dessert". This time I quickly surveyed what I had in the house, wrote down what else I needed to make banana bread, and hurried out the door.

My friend arrived and dinner was ready. I explained what was on the menu, I don't remember exactly, chicken and broccoli, I think. I then unveiled the banana bread and as I did, I excitedly exclaimed "AND banana bread!!!" She looked like she was in shock and asked if I was kidding. Right then I knew that, not only had I heard His voice, but there was something on it. She went on to explain that that exact morning the Lord had been asking her to write a list of things that she wanted. Guess what? Banana bread was one of the things on her list!

I had an encounter with His presence in the middle of making a grocery list. You can too! Just imagine all that is available to us as we invite His presence into all the seemingly menial tasks we do throughout the day.

Birthday Presents In His Presence

I don't know about you, but I like to give meaningful and functional gifts. Every time an occasion rolls around where gifts are given, I like to partner with Holy Spirit in finding the perfect gift, for the exact time at that exact moment in the person's life. It's actually really fun to go shopping with Holy Spirit.

My friend's birthday was a few weeks away and I had been pondering what to get her with Holy Spirit. I came up with a few ideas, but I just didn't quite feel "glory" on any of those ideas. One evening a few days before her birthday, I was in Target for something else when she came to mind, so I leaned in to see how Holy Spirit wanted to guide me. We walked through the new section by Chip and Joanna Gaines, but nothing stood out. The blanket section caught my eye and I headed over to see if we would find anything. After perusing a litany of blankets my eyes landed on a knitted cream blanket with a short fringe. I picked it up and leaned into Holy Spirit again. Without asking using words, I sensed that this was it. This was the birthday present we were going to get my friend.

Fast forward a few days and my friend shows up to the surprise party her husband and I had set up with a few close friends. She was definitely surprised, the cheesecake was amazing, and the time for presents had arrived. She opened several gifts before she got to mine and as soon as she opened the blanket she burst into tears. This blanket was the exact blanket that one of her co-workers had in her office and she had had her eye on it and been wanting one.

He knows our every thought! She hadn't even expressed out loud that she wanted that blanket. It was merely a thought in her mind. He wants to answer the ponderings in others hearts through your life. Will you let Him into the everyday details of your life?

Martha Is Mary

I was running errands one afternoon and had just checked out at Walmart. I was in bit of a hurry to get to a meeting and found myself standing in a line behind four or five people because at this particular Walmart they check receipts on the way out. Simultaneously, as I reached out to hand the attendant my receipt, I noticed her name was Martha and sensed the presence of God on her life. Without thinking, I opened my mouth and said, "Your name is Martha, but you're really a Mary". Her face lit up with a huge smile. She understood what that meant.

This was probably the shortest prophetic word I've ever given, but it was evident in her reaction that it touched a place in her heart. It's moments like these that I stand on the promise found in Psalm 81:10, "...open wide your mouth and I will fill it." I'm thankful that as I am moved by compassion for others that the Holy Spirit fills my mouth with His words that turn something like checking a receipt into an encounter.

Favorite Meal

I was texting with a friend when she got a call that her grandmother had just passed away unexpectedly. My friend lives in Texas, but she grew up in Canada where her grandmother had been living. When situations like this happen in life, we can either feel awkward or jump right in and be present. I chose the latter and told my friend I was going to bring dinner for her and her family.

I started thinking about what I could bring for dinner and weighing my schedule that day with cooking times and what her three children might like. I continued to ponder several ideas throughout my meetings and errands and was still undecided when I got to the grocery store that afternoon. When I ponder things it's as if I'm having a conversation with Holy Spirit, but without words.

I think of an idea and "lean" into it to get a sense if that feels like the best option or not. I will continue to ponder with Holy Spirit until I feel a peace or release on one option. I didn't have much time and as I stood in the deli section, I felt peace on a rotisserie chicken, so I grabbed one along with some bagged salad. As I stood waiting in the checkout line a clerk was stacking freshly baked loaves of bread. My friend and her family rarely eat bread, let alone glutenous white loaves of bread, but for some reason I grabbed a loaf and checked out. I got to my friend's house and started unloading the meal on the kitchen counter. When she saw what I had brought she exclaimed, "How did you know?" How did I know what? It turns out that rotisserie chicken with a baked loaf of white bread is one of their go to meals that the kids all like – praise Jesus!

Now it may seem a little overboard to have a conversation with Holy Spirit about what to eat for dinner, but I can guarantee you that my friend felt more loved in that moment than she would have if I had not asked. What could have been an ordinary dinner turned into an encounter with Love Himself. What could happen if you included Holy Spirit in all parts of your life, all day, every day?

Prompted by His Presence

I was walking out of a store when my attention was drawn to a woman who was on her way in, grabbing a cart. Before my brain caught up with my feet or mouth, I started walking towards her and got her attention. She turned towards me with a curious look as I proceeded to tell her that I sensed the presence of God radiating from her. My brain was still catching up to all that was happening when I saw a flash of a picture of her on a stage with a microphone. I described the picture I saw and asked if she happened to sing. She confirmed that she did, and I followed by asking if she sang on the worship team at church. She did. I immediately had a knowing, as if Father God was sharing His heart for her in that moment, that there was an anointing on her voice for breaking chains in people's lives as she sang. She thanked me for sharing and we both continued on our way.

I love that my awareness of His presence and leading can turn getting a grocery cart into an encounter. The Kingdom of God is available all the time every day, and we can tune into what Heaven is doing and pull it down in moments like these.

GRACE AND FAITH

Jesus tells us in John 6:44 (NIV) that, "No one can come to Me unless the Father who sent Me draws them..." It is the grace of God that reaches out and draws us in, but it is our faith that reaches back and accepts His grace that saves us. Romans 10:9 (NIV) reveals this truth, "If you declare with your mouth, 'Jesus is Lord,' and believe in your heart that God raised him from the dead, you will be saved."

Remember, John 6:44 teaches us that we cannot initiate having a relationship with God, He must first draw us to Himself. However, once we are saved, the connection that was broken by sin is immediately restored and we become His sons and daughters. Scripture is very clear about the access Jesus purchased for us on the cross in Ephesians 3:12 (NIV) "In Him and through faith in Him we may approach God with freedom and confidence," and in Ephesians 2:6 "And God raised us up with Christ and seated us with Him in the heavenly realms in Christ Jesus." We can approach God because we are seated in heaven with Christ. We have been given all access to Heaven...let that sink in for a minute...we have all been given full access to Heaven!

The truth that we have access to Heaven now is why we can live an everyday encounter lifestyle. What does that look like practically? Faith is the key to accessing all that is available to us in Heaven. We, as sons and daughters, can use our faith to pull down God's grace. Our position in Christ, as sons and daughters, allows us to initiate in our relationship with God. For example, we don't have to wait for God to lead us to pray for someone's healing. He is the Healer and we have access to His healing power as sons and daughters. Therefore, if someone needs healing, we can initiate praying for them because as sons and daughters we have access to

God's grace to heal.

I was standing in worship one day singing my lungs out to the lyrics of Show Me Your Glory. We got to the line "Show me Your glory, send down Your presence" when the Holy Spirit interrupted me and gently said, "I'm waiting on you." He then began to unravel the revelation of faith being the key to accessing His glory on earth.

Challenge yourself to step out, take risks, and use the access Jesus purchased on the cross. I promise you will experience everyday encounters!

ACTIVATION 1 – EXTENDING THE INVITATION
Instructions
Think about your day (or tomorrow if you are doing this in the evening). Invite Holy Spirit to join you for one specific task in your day. Ask Him to show you how He wants to be involved. Reflect on your experience after you have completed the activation.

What part of your day did you invite Holy Spirit into? Why?

_____

_____

_____

_____

_____

Describe Your Experience:

_____

_____

_____

_____

_____

_____

What other areas of life would you like to partner with Holy Spirit? Why?

_____

_____

_____

_____

_____

Takeaways from this Activation:

_____

_____

_____

_____

_____

ACTIVATION 2 – ACCESS BY FAITH
Instructions

Scripture reveals that God is our Healer. It is His nature to heal, therefore, we can conclude that we have access to healing because we have access to Him. Think of someone who needs healing. It could be a family member, friend, neighbor, or even yourself. Use your faith to access God's grace to heal and pray for that person. Your prayer can be short and simple, just like Jesus' healing prayers, or you can pray scripture over them. Ask the person to test (if possible) the ailment you have been praying for. Celebrate any improvements. Remember, we are not responsible for healing others, God is the Healer. If a person doesn't receive immediate healing, remind them that sometimes healing is a process. Leave them with hope that God is healing their bodies.

Who did you pray for?

_____

_____

What was their ailment?

_____

How did you feel going into this Activation?

_____
_____
_____
_____
_____

Describe Your Experience:

_____
_____
_____
_____
_____

Takeaways from this Activation:

_____
_____
_____
_____
_____

ACTIVATION 3 – TAKING A RISK
Instructions

Ask Holy Spirit to highlight someone in your social media feed. Once someone is highlighted, ask Holy Spirit for an answer to a question they have been asking. Share what you hear through a comment or message. Here is an example of a real-life testimony: A man asked Holy Spirit for a prophetic word for someone in his small group. He heard the word lemon and thought he was totally missing the mark. He took a risk and shared what he was hearing (lemon) and the man thanked him because he had been praying about whether or not to buy a certain car.

Make sure to ask for feedback from what you shared. Feedback helps us learn to discern when we are hearing correctly and when we're not. Remember, it's a learning process and we celebrate the risk not the results!

Who was highlighted? Did you know them?

_____

What answer did you hear when you asked Holy Spirit?

_____
_____
_____
_____
_____
_____
_____

Describe Your Experience:

_____
_____
_____
_____
_____
_____

Takeaways from this Activation:

_____
_____
_____
_____
_____
_____
_____

CHAPTER 3

CULTIVATING YOUR UNIQUE RELATIONSHIP

Relationship is the key to unlocking everyday encounters and it is important to understand that *your* relationship with Father God, Jesus, and Holy Spirit is unique. Of the billions of people across the globe, there is no one else exactly like you! Therefore, it would be impossible for your relationship with anyone to look exactly like someone else's relationship. It is literally impossible!

Imagine that I go to a coffee shop, order a latte, and sit down at the table with you. We have a conversation based on a list of ten questions. One hour later another friend shows up to the same coffee shop, orders the same latte, and sits down at the same table with you. You proceed to ask them the same ten questions, in the same order you asked me. Even though the atmosphere and content of the interactions were exactly the same, the experience you would have with each friend would be completely different...it's the same when we spend time in the presence of God.

Each of us brings our own unique experiences, thought processes, personality, likes, dislikes, joys, pains, and perspectives into every interaction in every relationship we have. When we hide or mute who we are our relational interactions are not truly genuine. Our relationship with God is no exception. God knows every hair on our head (Luke 12:7) and every thought we think (Psalm 139:4), but like any good parent or friend, it means more when the other person willingly communicates and is authentically themselves.

I want to challenge you to give yourself permission to be you, authentically you, in your relationship with Father God, Jesus, and Holy Spirit. Give yourself permission to be honest and real about your dreams, desires, struggles, and questions. I distinctly remember a moment when I chose to give myself full permission to be myself. I was spending time in my prayer closet. I had a literal prayer closet under the stairs that was specifically for spending time in God's presence. This particular day I was confronted with the reality of how I was feeling and my attempt to pray the right prayer. For years, I would honestly share my longings or desires with God and quickly finish my prayer with "...but if that's not Your best for me then I want Your best." It seemed like a valid, surrendered, honest prayer, but the Holy Spirit was confronting the mistrust at the root of my "humble" prayer. Psalm 37:4 (NIV) tells us to, "delight yourself in the Lord, and He will give you the desires of your heart." The ending of my prayer was really an escape clause that allowed me to believe that if what I wanted wasn't good enough for God that it must not be His best for me.

I made a choice that day and I shared my heart with the Lord. I chose to put myself out there, vulnerably before the Lord and trust Him with my actual desires. It was liberating. That one choice transformed my relationship with God. Instead of hoping that He would care, I started believing He already did. I gave myself permission to stop trying to pray the "right" prayers.

Be encouraged my friend! God is interested in His relationship with YOU! He is interested in spending time with YOU! He wants to engage with YOU the way you relate to Him. Give yourself permission and make the choices you need to make in order to fully experience your unique relationship with Father God, Jesus, and Holy Spirit. There is FREEDOM to be AUTHENTICALLY you!

TESTIMONIES
Dating Jesus

Starting in my mid-twenties I had several Valentine's Day encounters with Jesus. (You can read these Valentine's Day testimonies in my book Encounter Jesus: Cultivating Intimacy and Awareness) As a result of these encounters, a natural part of my unique relationship with Jesus has been to go on dates with Him.

You might be curious about what that looks like. John 1:1 tells us, "*In the beginning was the Word, and the Word was with God, and the Word was God,*" and John 1:14 goes on to say, "*The Word became flesh and made his dwelling among us.*" These scriptures tell us that Jesus is the Word of God. My dates with Jesus often look like going to a park, out for coffee, or specifically setting aside a night at home just with Him to spend time with Him in the Word of God.

Other times cultivating our relationship has been going to the movies, taking a day trip, sitting outside on the back porch admiring creation. Recently, I got home from work and was planning on knocking out some administrative tasks for a class I help with at church. I got out my computer and all the documents and as I turned to start typing, I heard that still small voice, "Let's go look at houses." In that moment, I had a choice to prioritize my relationship with Him or get some work done. I chose to grab my keys, hop in the car, and take a drive. The conversation that afternoon in the car was good, but what was more important, was that I invested in the relationship.

Relationships are about give and take. They require communication and input from both parties in order to be a healthy thriving relationship. I'm thankful that the invitation works both ways!

Finding Your Spot

Judy Franklin, Bill Johnson's previous personal assistant at Bethel Church in Redding, California, came to speak at my church in Florida. That weekend she shared encounters that she had experienced going to Heaven and led us through several encounters. During one encounter, she asked us to picture Jesus in front of us. I immediately saw myself sitting across from Jesus at a white wrought iron table for two. Jesus would ask me questions, and I would reply, neither of us using words. Since that encounter the white wrought iron garden table has been one of the "spots" where I will spend time encountering Jesus and cultivating our relationship.

In any relationship, whether friendship, romantic, or family, we make memories and those memories become some of our favorite "spots." We can apply this same relational principle to our relationship with Father God, Jesus, and Holy Spirit. I often spend time with Father God sitting on the edge of a circular fountain in the middle of a garden. We sit side by side with our feet in the water and talk. When I spend time with Holy Spirit, I often see Him sitting on my right shoulder in the form of a dove (Luke 3:22 NIV). Ephesians 3:20 tells us that, "...He will do immeasurably more than all we ask or imagine" and 1 Corinthians 2:16 reminds us, "we have the mind of Christ." Therefore, it is completely scriptural to use our mind's imagination to explore and experience our relationship with Father God, Jesus, and Holy Spirit. I encourage you to spend time with them and allow them to connect with you in your imagination!

Vacation Time

I prioritize my relationship with God. I treat it like any other relationship. I intentionally carve out time each day during the week to spend time together. As you've read, I also go out on dates to prioritize and spend time cultivating my relationship with Father God, Jesus, and Holy Spirit.

A few years ago, I decided I wanted to take a vacation with the purpose of spending time with Father God, Jesus, and Holy Spirit. I wanted to get away and spend some extended time with Him. As a single woman I had to use wisdom in making my vacation plans. Camping in the middle of woods alone wouldn't have been very wise! I decided to spend a week in Redding, California. Bethel Church is in Redding and they have multiple services, along with an amazing prayer room and garden. They also have security around the clock to make sure it is safe.

I want to share some of the plans and details of the trip to give an example of what it has looked like for me to cultivate my relationship with Him. I didn't plan the trip and ask Him to join me, I planned the entire trip with Him. I gathered the service times, local attractions, and schedule of other events at the church and partnered with Holy Spirit to see what He was highlighting for the trip. I even invited Holy Spirit into choosing the hotel, which airport to fly into, and what kind of car to rent. He knows everything…and He even led me to some deals!

I woke up one morning about two weeks before the trip. I was in that half-awake-half-asleep state when I heard that still small voice says, "I want you to write a book in Hebrews (the coffee shop at Bethel) while you're in Redding." He then proceeded to give me a download of the title and chapters for the book. Never in my life had I ever planned on writing a book, but when you are in a relationship it allows the other party to make suggestions and offer ideas. The day before I left for the trip, He shared that He wanted to spend time together in the prayer house from 2-4am. It was an amazing trip and I was able to write the entire first draft of the book in the week I was there.

Again, I share this testimony and these details to show that relationship is truly that - a partnership between two people that do life together.

How Do You Hear Him?

Hearing the voice of God is critical in your relationship with Him. God is always speaking. He sent the Holy Spirit to be our Counselor, Helper, and Guide. Communication is necessary for anyone to be a counselor, helper, or guide and this also rings true for our relationship with God.

Many of us question if we hear God's voice, but that is the wrong question. The question is not "Is God speaking?", the question is "How does God speak to me?" The answer is that God speaks to each one of us uniquely and individually. He speaks through hearing, feeling, seeing, sensing, knowing, and even smelling!

Learning to hear God's voice was an interesting process for me. My prayer life has always looked like me asking a lot of questions and listening for His answer. Initially, I would ask a question and read the bible to "hear" His answer. Then I began asking questions when I was praying, and I would immediately hear an answer in the form of a voice inside my head. The answers would almost come immediately, and it seemed too easy to really be God speaking to me. I decided to practice listening so I could actually hear God's voice, and after a week of practice I realized that I really had been hearing His voice the whole time.

The one mistake I made in learning to hear God's voice was comparing myself to others. I was trying to learn how it worked, and I found that it's not a formula. Just like you might be serious with one friend and silly with another, how each individual communicates with God is different. When I would ask friends how they heard from God they would describe feeling His presence, so for a long time I didn't think I could hear God's voice because I wasn't feeling anything. It took a few years to realize that there were many ways to hear from God.

Will you give yourself permission to hear from God the way He speaks to you?

Reality Check

I remember some friends who were sick on their wedding day. In fact, they were so sick they had to stop by the drugstore on the way to the hotel. I'm pretty sure that the stop at the drugstore after leaving the wedding wasn't something they had imagined. I have another friend who went to IKEA the morning after her wedding to use some gift cards before they left on their honeymoon. I'm pretty sure that neither of these couples wedding day dreams included stops at the drugstore or IKEA. The point is that real life doesn't play out like the movies, real life is just that…real!

Our relationship with God also happens in the context of real life. I honestly use to think that if I did "it" right, whatever that really means, that eventually my time spent in God's presence would include the Heavens parting, angels descending, and harps playing in the background. Well, not exactly that elaborate, but I had expectations of what my relationship with God should look like in order to prove I had arrived. You could say I had a "blockbuster-hit-movie" expectation of what my relationship with God would look like. The reality is that God our relationship with God also happens in real life. There are ups, downs, highs, and lows. It's real!

In October 2017 I moved from Florida to Austin, Texas to be a part of the Bethel Austin Church. I packed my car and my cat and drove fourteen hours west to a city I had never been before. To make the move even more adventurous, I also didn't know anyone. It was an exciting season, but a season filled with lots of transition. It was in the season that I truly learned to be authentic with God. Over the years I had cultivated my relationship with the Lord. I spent time in the Word of God and in His presence, but I had never experienced that much transition before in my life. Some days I would go into the prayer closet, and because I had spent all my energy meeting new people or figuring out where to register my car, the only energy I had left was to fall asleep in His presence. I was rather critical of my behavior initially; however, the Lord began to speak to me. "What parent wouldn't melt at their child falling asleep in their lap?" I was undone.

Talk about reality check?! He wasn't disappointed in my lack of energy. He was delighted that even when I had no energy I would still come. Give yourself permission to be real with God. He can handle it, and it will take your relationship to a deeper level of intimacy!

KNOW YOUR SEASON

Ecclesiastes 3:1 (NIV) teaches us, "There is a time for everything, and a season for every activity under the heavens." Seasons are important to understand in relationship too. What does your current season look like? Are things vibrant and blissful like summer? Are things beginning to die and fall to the wayside like autumn? Are you experiencing the barrenness and hibernation of winter? Are you in a season of spring time when new life is beginning to burst forth? Seasons are important because if we try to plant in a season of barrenness the return won't be very fruitful.

It may seem that some seasons are better than others, but the truth is that each season is necessary for growth. There are seasons where you find favor at every turn and seasons where there is no favor at all. Remember, Ecclesiastes 3:1 (NIV) says, *"There is a time for everything, and a season for every activity under the heaven,"* and He put it in the bible so that we would know that life is made up of seasons.

A few years ago, I experienced an unexpected season shift. From the time I graduated from high school I had never actually applied for a job. My entire life, up until this point, jobs had been offered to me, created for me, or I knew someone who helped me get my foot in the door. In the spring of 2013, the grant I had been coordinating ended. The college I was working for created a position to continue the program, but due to recent changes in employment laws they could only offer the position at 25 hours per week. This was the beginning of a long season of favor lifting in my life. I spent a year and a half in that position and just wasn't able to support myself, so I began applying for full time jobs and turned in my resignation. I began teaching again as an adjunct professor and was making more money teaching two college courses for six hours a week than I had been making working 25 hours a week. I began applying for jobs and shortly began receiving rejection letter after rejection letter. It was rough. I couldn't figure out what I had done wrong. I loved God, I was serving Him, and I didn't understand how my padded resume and 10+ years of experience weren't enough for even an interview. What I understand now but didn't then was that the season had shifted. In hindsight, I can see how the Lord was beginning the process of moving me to Texas after living in Florida my entire life. Moving was not on my radar. I was planted with deep roots and my only plans to leave were for vacations.

Not all season shifts are as massive as moving your life half way across the country, but this story is a good example of Isaiah 55:8-9, "For My thoughts are not your thoughts, neither are your ways My ways, declares the Lord. As the heavens are higher than the earth, so are My ways higher than your ways and My thoughts than your thoughts." His thoughts and ways are higher than ours. He knows the plans He has for us and they are plans to prosper and not to harm us (Jeremiah 29:11 NIV). It's so important that you are in tune with the Lord and discerning the season you are in. Trust me, it will save you a lot of doubt and questioning. Having been through a major season shift I've learned to trust that He is working all things together for my good (Romans 8:28).

Before I end this section, I want to share another revelation about seasons I've learned along my journey. There are seasons for sowing and seasons for reaping. Too many times I've sown my bread (what was meant to nourish me) in Jesus' name only to see it rot in the proverbial ground. Farmers don't take bread and plant it in the ground, that's crazy! If it is crazy to do in the natural, why not adopt the same principle in the spiritual? Conversely, if we eat our seed rather than sowing it, we rob ourselves of the multiplied fruit that seed was designed to produce. Again, we must know our season in order to flourish in the Kingdom. Holy Spirit is our Counselor and Guide and will lead us into all truth (John 16:13). He can help us discern the season we are in through relationship!

TOOLS FOR CULTIVATING RELATIONSHIP

The most important thing in any relationship is communication. Father God has given us Himself, in Jesus, the Word of God and Holy Spirit, who is the Spirit of God, for cultivating relationship with Him. There are denominations that exist within the Christian Church that focus only on the Word of God and others that keep their focus mainly on the Spirit of God. The truth is…we were given both for a reason. Jesus is the Word made flesh. When we spend time in the Word of God we are spending time with a person, Jesus. When we invite Holy Spirit into our time with Jesus, the Word of God, He speaks to us, not just what was said, but what He is saying in that specific moment. They work together. The same is true for our time spent in the presence of God with Holy Spirit. The encounters, visions, dreams, and revelations we receive in these times should be in line with the truth found in the Word of God. Jesus and Holy Spirit are always in agreement. When we spend time the presence God what we experience will always agree with the Word of God.

Time spent with Jesus, who is the Word of God, and Holy Spirit in the presence of God are the most important parts of cultivating our relationship with God. All other tools for cultivating relationship are supportive and should never become more important than God Himself. I remember discipling a college student who was rather distraught with the amount of time she felt like she had to spend reading her bible. I asked her to elaborate on her dilemma. She went on to explain that she was spending time reading the bible every day, but that she wasn't reading "enough" and it was causing her to feel guilty. Partnering with Holy Spirit I discerned that reading her bible had actually become an idol. I asked her if she thought reading her bible every day for a specific amount of time has become an idol. As soon as I asked the question, something broke over her life. In that moment, she physically experienced the release of the guilt she had been carrying, and revelation broke through. Was she reading a book as a task or spending time getting to know the person of Jesus the Word of God? It was a beautiful moment and her life hasn't been the same since.

Tools aren't bad – a bible, journal, phone apps, podcasts, etc. – they can be used to help cultivate our relationship with God, but they should never replace engaging with the God Himself. Be encouraged to explore your relationship with Father God, Jesus, and Holy Spirit. Do things you've never done. Spend time with them places you never have before. Engage in ways you've never tried. It's a relationship and there is freedom in healthy relationships!

ACTIVATION 1 – Q&A
Instructions
Write down a list of questions you have about your season. First, ask your questions to Father God. Next, ask the same questions to Jesus. Finally, ask the same questions to Holy Spirit. Make sure to take your time and listen to what each has to say. Take time to reflect on your experience after you have completed the activation.

What questions did you ask?

_____
_____
_____
_____
_____
_____
_____

Describe your experience with Father God:

_____

_____

_____

_____

_____

Describe your experience with Jesus:

_____

_____

_____

_____

_____

Describe your experience with Holy Spirit:

_____

_____

_____

_____

_____

How was each interaction similar? Different?

_____

_____

_____

_____

_____

Takeaways from this Activation:

_____

_____

_____

_____

_____

ACTIVATION 2 – CULTIVATING RELATIONSHIP
Instructions

Choose an activity you would like to do. Throughout the activity spend specific segments of time with Father God, Jesus, and Holy Spirit. (For example, I may choose to go to the park. I might walk around the lake with Father God, swing on the swing with Jesus, and sit at the picnic table with Holy Spirit.) The purpose is to spend time cultivating your unique relationship with Father God, Jesus, and the Holy Spirit. Take time to reflect on your experience after you have completed the activation.

What activity did you choose? Why?

_____

_____

_____

_____

_____

Describe your experience with Father God:

_____

_____

_____

_____

_____

Describe your experience with Jesus:

_____

_____

_____

_____

_____

_____

_____

Describe your experience with Holy Spirit:

_____
_____
_____
_____
_____

How was each interaction similar? Different?

_____
_____
_____
_____
_____

Takeaways from this Activation:

_____
_____
_____
_____
_____

ACTIVATION 3 – TAKING A RISK
Instructions
Schedule a time to spend with God doing something that is outside of your comfort zone. The goal here is to spend time with Him doing something outside of your normal "quite time" routine.

What did you decide to do? Why?

_____
_____
_____
_____
_____

How did you feel going into the experience?

_____

_____

_____

_____

_____

Describe your experience:

_____

_____

_____

_____

Takeaways from this Activation:

_____

_____

_____

_____

_____

_____

_____

_____

_____

_____

_____

_____

_____

_____

_____

_____

_____

_____

CHAPTER 4

SERVANT VS. FRIEND

How do you approach God? I distinctly remember a moment when God spoke profoundly to me during worship one day. I had my eyes closed with my head tilted up towards the ceiling, singing my guts out. Then He spoke, "I'm not up there, I'm right in front of you." I was singing up at Him while He was standing right in front of me, face to face. My posture indicated what I believed about my relationship with God – there was distance between us. James 4:8 (TPT) tells us, "*Move your heart closer and closer to God, and He will come even closer to you.*" Ephesians 3:12 (NIV) tells us, "*In Him and through faith in Him we may approach God with freedom and confidence.*" I was approaching Him with a servant mindset when Jesus makes our position clear in John 15:15 (NIV), "*I no longer call you servants, because a servant does not know his master's business. Instead, I have called you friends, for everything that I learned from my Father I have made known to you.*"

There is a big difference between a servant and a friend. Servants take orders, friends get to have input. Servants are submissive, friends are seen as equals. Servants have limited access, friends have full access. Servants need permission, friends are given freedom. John 15:15 in The Passion Translation describes the difference between a servant and a friend the best, "*I have never called you 'servants,' because a master doesn't confide in his servants, and servants don't always understand what the master is doing. But I call you my most intimate friends, for I reveal to you everything that I've heard from my Father.*" A master doesn't confide in his servants because servants don't understand, but Jesus shared everything He learned with us because He calls us His most intimate friends!

Let me ask the question again, how do you approach God? Is it from a servant perspective or as one of His intimate friends? Intimate friends can be confident in their position in the relationship and bold in sharing from the security of that place. I challenge you to examine your relationship with God and see how you approach Him. Know that it is possible to be a confident friend in some areas, while servant minded in others.

The intimacy of friendship is vital to unlocking everyday encounters. Jesus made the way for us to be fully one with God and filled with the Holy Spirit. Believe and fully receive the friendship

He offers us through the cross. It is not arrogance to receive and walk in all that Jesus purchased for us. Will you be His intimate friend?

TESTIMONIES
Soldier On

I learned that I was a friend of God the hard way. I distinctly remember a moment at a women's retreat. I was standing in front of a woman who was praying for me and internally I remember turning my attention to the Lord and praying, "I'll do whatever you want me to do" and I meant it with all my heart. The irony of this prayer is that I was praying from a servant mentality. I didn't know that I was praying from that perspective, it was a heartfelt genuine prayer, but the Lord was about to take me on the journey into the revelation that I actually have access as His intimate friend who lives face to face with Him.

He began speaking to me through a math equation that I learned in algebra, $y = mx + b$. He began to explain that if this was the "equation of life" I was leaving out a very crucial variable – me! Remember how I told Him I would do whatever He wanted? Well, He was showing me that my prayer didn't fit the equation. I was leaving what I wanted out of it. This is the difference between a servant and a friend. Servants obey, friends have a say in the relationship. This was the beginning of learning how to engage the Lord as His friend.

We must include ourselves – our wants and desires – in our relationship with the Lord. If we don't offer ourselves in our vulnerability, then we're just His servants and we cheat Him of what He purchased on the cross! Let's give Jesus His full reward by walking in friendship with Him!

Time to Move

I was in worship one evening at the opening sessions of a weekend long conference, and out of nowhere I heard the Holy Spirit whisper, "It's time to move." Move? Who me? I'd lived in

Florida my entire life. After graduating from high school, I moved to Tallahassee, Florida to attend college – twice – and ended up staying. I had been in Tallahassee for 19 years and I had no intentions of going anywhere. A few months prior, I was visiting Bethel Church in Redding, California. One morning as I walked through the prayer garden, the Holy Spirit said to me, "Don't move to Redding." I replied, "Don't worry. I won't. I'm not going anywhere."

The "fun" part about feeling led to move was that I had no direction for where to move. He did not include that in the instructions! I wanted to partner with what He was saying so I began asking questions in our times together. I also made a list of leaders and places across the country that had the same DNA and things I wanted in a church and city. Months went by, nothing. A few more months, nothing. Then one day, four months after being announced, I ran across a Facebook post saying that Bethel Church in Redding was going to be planting a church in Austin. My heart leaped and I began researching to figure out the what, when, and where. One of the things my searching uncovered was a Facebook group for people interested in Bethel Austin, along with videos of the leaders sharing vision and information about the church plant. I would watch them and ask God, "What about Austin?" Nothing. Just crickets. I didn't hear an answer or get an impression either way. This went on for two weeks. By this time, I had caught up on all the informational meeting videos and filled out an interest form to get updates as they moved forward. One morning in my office I couldn't take it anymore and I said out loud, "I want to go to Austin!" That evening while at dinner, my pastor texted me and asked if I could host the team that was coming with Steve Backlund, who is one of the leaders at Bethel in Redding. Confirmation finally came, but it was only after I voiced what I wanted to God.

In hindsight, I realized that this whole process was God inviting me into friendship with Him. Up until this point I was really good at hearing from Him and obeying what He said, but Jesus didn't die for us to be obedient slaves. He died to restore the friendship that God had with Adam and Eve when He walked with them in the cool of the day (Generis 3:8 NIV). He wanted to know what I wanted because I am his friend!

How Would You Ask?

One morning a few months after I had moved to Austin, I was sitting in the prayer closet spending time with Jesus. In this particular season I was struggling with believing that God's promises for me would really happen. There are some things I have been contending for for years. Somehow, it always seems so much easier to believe and have faith for others, and I was lovingly being confronted with the struggle in my own heart. After a while, I turned on a podcast by Seth Dahl. I don't remember exactly what the topic of the podcast was, but I vividly remember an illustration he used that immediately broke the powerless moment I was having. He was sharing a story about a time one of his kids asked him for something. His child was whining and kept asking over and over again. Seth's response to his child's behavior is what blew my mind. He turned to his whining child and said, "How would you ask me if you believed I wanted to give it to you?"

It's safe to say that my prayer life shifted in that moment. Friends don't whine for things that they want or need from their friends. They simply ask, believing!

Establishing the Kingdom

I work for a non-profit that partners churches with elementary schools and helps pair volunteers from the churches to read with the students. I also have the opportunity to read with two third grade boys once a week on Thursday mornings. Recently I took a picture of the school's sign where I read and posted it to my Instagram account (Follow me @beencountered). I posted it with the following caption, "Today the Kingdom was established here because I showed up. We can have CONFIDENCE because of the PROMISE in Joshua 1:3 (NIV) - I will give you EVERY place where you set your foot. Where did YOU go today? ...It MATTERS because you CARRY God's Presence whenever you go!!!"

I am able to make such a bold statement because I know who I am and Whose I am. A servant would never make such a bold statement. We must be confident in our friendship with God so that we can go make disciples (Matthew 28:19 NIV), heal the sick, raise the dead, cleanse the lepers, drive out demons (Matthew 10:8 NIV), and "do greater things" (John 14:12 NIV). Friends know their access and authority in the Kingdom!

Pray for Healing?

I've always been more comfortable prophesying over someone than I have been for praying for their healing - until recently. 1 Corinthians 12 (NIV) outlines all the spiritual gifts and teaches us in verse 11 that, "*He (Holy Spirit) distributes them to each one, just as He determines,*" so I always thought that because I could operate in the prophetic that that was the gift I had been given and healing just wasn't something I had been given. I was wrong.

I am a friend of the Most High God and I have the Holy Spirit living inside of me (Ephesians 1:13). When I got saved and the Holy Spirit came to live inside of me I didn't just get part of the Holy Spirit, I got all of Him; which includes the part of His nature that heals! I was basing my access to Him off of my experience and not off of His character. Having shifted my perspective and operating from a place of friendship, I am now starting to see people get healed when I pray. The same power that raised Christ from the dead lives in me and I have access to it as His friend!

CONFIDENCE VS ARROGANCE

Religion teaches that we are sinners and gives us rules to follow, however, in the Kingdom of God we are saints and invited into an intimate relationship with Father God, Jesus, and Holy Spirit. We've read in Ephesians 3:12 (NIV) that we can "*approach God with freedom and confidence,*" and it's actually true! Kris Vallotton says, "Confidence always looks like arrogance to the insecure!" Think about that. What is your response to someone who walks confidently in the Kingdom, knowing that they are a son or daughter of the Most

High God? Are you inspired? Are you encouraged? Do you feel insecure? Do you get intimidated? The healthy response is to celebrate all that God is doing in and through our brothers and sisters. We are each created in the image of God (Genesis 1:27 NIV) which means that every person is a reflection of the image of God. What we see in and through others' lives is a glimpse of all that is available in the Kingdom of God for all believers. We can compare or we can celebrate.

Give others permission to be fully alive and confident in their identity in Christ. Don't mistake someone's confidence in who they are in Christ for arrogance. When we know who we are and Whose we are, the natural response should be security and confidence. Jesus got the keys to our Heavenly identity on the cross. He became the Way, the Truth, and the Life in order to lead us into an abundant life, which includes being confident sons and daughters!

ACTIVATION 1 – FRIENDSHIP WITH GOD
Instructions

Set aside some time to spend specifically with Father God. Write down some questions about your friendship and spend some time listening to His answers. Make sure you have something to write down what you discuss in your conversation. Reflect on your experience after you have completed the activation.

What questions did you ask?

_____
_____
_____
_____
_____

Describe your experience with Father God:

_____
_____
_____
_____

What did you learn about your friendship with Father God?

_____

_____

_____

_____

_____

Takeaways from this Activation:

_____

_____

_____

_____

_____

ACTIVATION 2 – FRIENDSHIP WITH JESUS
Instructions
Meditate on John 15:15. Read it in several translations. Invite Jesus to confide in you. Ask Him to reveal something to you that He's heard from the Father. Take time to reflect on your encounter after you have completed the activation.

What was your favorite translation of John 15:15? Why?

_____

_____

_____

_____

_____

Describe your experience with Jesus:

_____

_____

_____

_____

_____

What did you learn about your friendship with Jesus?

_____

_____

_____

_____

_____

Takeaways from this Activation:

_____

_____

_____

_____

_____

ACTIVATION 3 – FRIENDSHIP WITH HOLY SPIRIT
Instructions

Holy Spirt is out Comforter and Guide. Set some time aside to partner with your friend, Holy Spirit, to pray for someone. The purpose of this activation is for you to initiate and choose someone you would like to pray for. Ask Holy Spirit to give you an encouraging word for the person you choose. Share what Holy Spirit reveals with the person you chose. Remember to get feedback. Take time to reflect on this experience below.

How did you feel initiating with Holy Spirit? Why?

_____

_____

_____

_____

_____

Describe your experience:

_____

_____

_____

Takeaways from this Activation:

_____

_____

_____

_____

_____

_____

_____

_____

_____

_____

_____

_____

_____

_____

_____

_____

_____

_____

_____

_____

_____

_____

_____

_____

_____

_____

_____

_____

_____

_____

_____

_____

CHAPTER 5
PARTNERING IN EVERYDAY LIFE

When we believe and receive Jesus as our Lord and Savior, we enter into covenant with Him; we enter into an eternal relationship. We become His friend. We must live with this truth in mind. When we do, we can partner with Him in everyday life and access the fullness of all He designed and desires our relationship to be. To partner with God means to be together with Him in life, all day, every day. It's simple, just live your life together with God. Which parts of life? Every…single…part.

In my first book, Encounter Jesus: Cultivating Awareness and Intimacy, I give five keys for having encounters and provide thirty encounter activations. This second book is designed to help solidify partnership with Father God, Jesus, and Holy Spirit throughout each day. When I was a new Christian, I read a book that was talking about the verse in 1 Thessalonians 5:17 that says, "pray without ceasing." I remember thinking about how impossible it would be to make a list long enough and be focused enough to constantly pray all day every day. My concept of prayer at that time was limited to writing down requests and praying through the list over and over and over. I've matured over the years as I've grown in friendship with Father God, Jesus, and Holy Spirit. I now have revelation that "prayer without ceasing" is more of a constant awareness of His presence throughout my day. It's the revelation that moved me from a servant's mindset to the reality of friendship with Him.

I invite you to partner with Him all day, every day. It's a process. Give yourself permission to be in process because process is one of God's greatest gifts, and He'll be there with you right in the middle of it. I still have moments when I realize I haven't been aware of His presence in several hours, but the more I spend time in His presence the more I am aware of it. I had to be alone in a quiet room. I am so familiar with His voice and His presence that I can sense subtle nudges when I'm fully focused on another task or in public. It's possible. Give it time. Give yourself grace. He does!

TESTIMONIES
Waking Up

As soon as I hear the alarm go off in the morning my internal dialog with Him starts. The best way I can describe our conversations is like that of a spouse or a best friend. You know, those relationships where you give them one glance and in that glance you had a ten minute conversation without any words. It's definitely taken time to grow in friendship, but this is now the level of intimacy I experience with Him on a regular basis. Our morning conversation goes through the tasks of the morning – breakfast, shower, exercise, time together – we decide an order and I hop out of bed. I often use my time exercising or in the shower to make declarations, ask Him questions, or worship.

I typically spend time with Father God, Jesus, and Holy Spirit in the mornings. I have my bible, journal, communion, and several books on the table next to me. The internal conversation goes on, "What do you want to do today? What do you want to do first?" It's a partnership. It may seem intense or extreme, but I've spent years cultivating intimacy and awareness in relationship with Him and at this point in my life it just naturally flows. He is my partner in life. We do everything together! He wants the same with you!

Crowned

I had to get a crown. No, not the shiny kind that queens and kings wear, but the kind that goes on your tooth. I waited several years and took extremely good care of my large filling in hopes that I wouldn't have to get a crown, but alas, the day arrived. I've gone to the dentist my whole life and even had braces, but there is just something a little unnerving about having needles being in your mouth. I'll spare the rest of the details, but I want to share how I partnered with God in this situation.

I've never had a crown before, so I wasn't sure what to expect. I called the office the week before to get more information, but they were closed for the entire week. My appointment was one hour after the office opened on Monday morning so there wasn't much time to get details. I called right when they opened, and the receptionist did her best to explain the procedure. For some reason, it helps me to have an idea of things that are about to happen to me! I wasn't afraid, I just like to be informed. I sat down in the dentist chair and immediately invited Holy Spirit to come, Jesus the Prince of Peace to be present in the room, and I leaned into their presence. Less than a minute later the hygienist took my blood pressure which came back at 109/69. She went on to comment that most patients' blood pressure is usually higher at the dentist office, but mine was one of the lowest she'd seen. She didn't know I wasn't there alone. His presence shifts atmospheres and He lives inside of me...even at the dentist!

Dishes with Jesus

I went to visit a friend in England for a few weeks to hang out and spend some time at a few ministry meetings with her. This woman is amazing. She's in her 70s and operates like she's in her 20s. She travels all over the city and the country carrying the presence of God wherever she goes. I had no other agenda other than to spend time with her doing whatever she was doing because I wanted to glean from her experience and atmosphere. I firmly believe that if you want to fly you have to hang out with eagles, not chickens.

One night during the trip I was washing dishes after we had eaten dinner. I had no intention of doing anything other than washing the dishes, but when you are in relationship with Father God, Jesus, and Holy Spirit they tend to treat it just as it is, a relationship. As I stood there washing the dishes, Holy Spirit began speaking to me about a meeting we would be attending the next day. He showed me a picture of a ground swell and then described what it represented. I finished washing dishes and shared it with my friend. She confirmed that what I had seen and heard made sense and we went on with our evening. The next morning at the meeting she unexpectedly invited me to share with the group. As I shared, the presence of God filled the room and many were touched in His presence that morning. I'm so glad I did the dishes! Where does God want to meet you during your day?

Write a Book?

Writing a book was never on my radar – ever! Here I am in the middle of writing my second book. Why? Because I'm in partnership with God and He thought it would be a good idea if we wrote a book together. Doing something I never desired or imagined doing has actually been really fun and easy. Working in partnership with God makes the impossible possible. What I wouldn't do on my own, I have done because I am in partnership!

When I write, we write together. Up until this morning, I only had the outline through this chapter. When I sat down to spend time with God I asked what He wanted to talk about today. I went to grab my bible and felt Him saying, "Let's just have coffee." I picked up my coffee, began sipping, and focused on listening to what He wanted to say. I didn't know what He was going to share, but we've cultivated our relationship long enough to allow us to decide together. It's so important that we listen for His voice instead of trying to think about what He might to say. As I listened, He slowly began to download an entire second section for this book. I don't know how to write books, but together we do!

What does He want to do with you in partnership? What is He inviting you into? I encourage you to make room in your relationship for Him to share some of the dreams He wants to do with you – together!

Finding Time

Growing up, my parents would wake up at 5:15am to spend time together before us four girls started waking up. It was a partnership and they prioritized spending time together. Our relationship with God isn't any different. My parents figured out a time to spend time together that worked for their specific season of life; four young girls under the age of five. It's important to remember that you will go through seasons in your relationship with God and the time that you spend with Him will probably look different in different seasons, but it doesn't mean it isn't important or valuable to Him.

I typically wake up early to make sure I have at least one hour and thirty minutes to spend with Him in the morning. I know this isn't possible in all seasons of life, and I want to share some of the other creative times I've come up with for spending time with God. I basically like to invite Him into whatever I'm doing, especially when what I'm doing doesn't require full attention. Some of my best conversations and revelations have come while taking a shower or driving in the car. I'll also use the times doing these activities to worship or make declarations. Another time I like to ponder things with Holy Spirit is when I'm blow drying my hair. There is something about the noise that drowns out all other noises and helps me to focus on Him. I've also been known to talk to Him while I'm brushing my teeth, folding laundry, or working out.

Like I said before, find time to spend with Him that works for the current season in your life. Give yourself grace to be flexible and know that you don't have to be sitting still, for a fixed amount of time, every day to have a quality relationship and partnership with God. Our relationship with Him is just like any other relationship. Is it important to have one-on-one, completely focused time with one another? Yes! Does that mean that any other time spent together doesn't count? No! There is freedom! Give yourself permission to stop judging the time you spend with God as "good" or "bad" and begin to see all time spent with Him as valuable.

Matthew 12:34 (NIV) says, "The mouth speaks what the heart is full of." If you want to see the quality of your relationship with God, just take note when life gives you a squeeze. When an orange is squeezed what is inside comes out. When life squeezes you what comes out? One time my cat, Hammy P. Cat, was chasing me around the house, and I tripped on my pajama pants and smashed my knee into the ground. The moment I smashed my knee into the ground, I heard myself cry out, "Jesus" as if asking Him to heal whatever just got hurt. Life had just squeezed me and what was inside came out. This didn't happen because I chose my words carefully in the moment, but instead it was my automatic response because of the relationship I've spent time cultivating.

Be encouraged that there is time within every day for you to connect and build relationship with God. He doesn't judge the amount of time, He is delighted that you come!

THERE IS FREEDOM

I can't tell you what partnering with Father God, Jesus, and Holy Spirit will look like for you because every relationship is different. Communication, desires, interests, and seasons are all different for each individual. There is no one right way to partner with God, there is only your way of doing it!

Galatians 5:1 says, *"It is for freedom that Christ has set us free. Stand firm, then, and do not let yourselves be burdened again by a yoke of slavery."* It is for freedom that Christ set us free and that includes freedom in relationship. Religion is the "yoke of slavery" that binds us with do's and don'ts. Be free! Be you! Spend time with Him the way you want to spend time with Him, and give room for Him to share how He wants to spend time with you. There is freedom!

ACTIVATION 1 – ERRANDS
Instructions
The next time do you do errands, make a conscious effort to invite and be aware of Holy Spirit. Ask questions. Listen for His responses. Reflect on your experience after you have completed the activation.

What errands did you do with Holy Spirit?

_____
_____
_____
_____
_____

How were these errands different from other errands without Him?

_____
_____
_____
_____
_____

In what other every day area(s) of life would you like to partner with Him? Why?

_____
_____
_____
_____
_____

Takeaways from this Activation:

_____
_____
_____
_____
_____

ACTIVATION 2 – DISCOVERING YOUR "BOOK"
Instructions
Just like God wanted to write a book with me, set aside some time to ask God to share a dream He as for the two of you. Reflect on this encounter after you have completed the activation.

What dream did God show you?

_____
_____
_____
_____

What was your initial reaction to what He shared? Why?

_____

_____

_____

_____

_____

What about this dream makes you excited? Scared?

_____

_____

_____

_____

_____

What is one step you can take in the next week to move towards this dream?

_____

_____

_____

_____

_____

Takeaways from this Activation:

_____

_____

_____

_____

_____

ACTIVATION 3 – DECISION MAKING
Instructions
Write down a list of ten decisions you need to make. No decision is too little or too big. Choose one to partner with Holy Spirit and begin a dialogue about this decision. Remember to ask questions and take time to listen. Reflect on this process below.

What decision did you choose to make with Holy Spirit? Why?

_____

_____

_____

_____

_____

_____

_____

_____

_____

_____

Describe your experience:

_____

_____

_____

_____

_____

_____

_____

_____

_____

Takeaways from this Activation:

_____

_____

_____

_____

_____

_____

_____

_____

_____

SECTION TWO

CHAPTER 6
GETTING STARTED

Revelation 12:11 (NKJV) says, *"And they overcame him (satan) by the blood of the Lamb and by the word of their testimony."* The content of this entire section is comprised solely of activations based on encounters I have experienced personally or led others through directly. You will receive breakthrough as you go through each encounter and will step into deeper intimacy and relationship with Father God, Jesus, and Holy Spirit. How can I be this confident? I am standing on the promise in Revelation 12:11 that we overcome by the blood of the Lamb and the word of our testimony. If every encounter in this section is a testimony, then you will overcome as you complete these activations. Stand on this promise and have expectancy of breakthrough and freedom!

REMINDERS FOR ENCOUNTERS
Use Your Imagination

When you are prompted to ask a question or imagine something don't think, use your imagination. Ephesians 3:20 (NIV) encourages us that God can *"do immeasurably more than all we ask or imagine…"* and 1 Corinthians 2:16 tells us *"we have the mind of Christ."* Therefore, we can confidently use our minds and imaginations when we have encounters with Father God, Jesus, and Holy Spirit.

Sometimes when praying for people they question if what they heard was really from God. More often than not, what they heard was God. Give yourself permission and stand on these promises. Trust that you actually do hear God speaking to you. Romans 8:1 (NIV) is also a great filter to test what you are hearing during an encounter, *"There is therefore now no condemnation for those who are in Christ Jesus."* If what you are hearing feels condemning, then it's probably not God. We can trust the Word of God because it is literally Jesus (John 1:1,14 NIV)!

Listen, Don't Think

Listening is key when having encounters. Thinking introduces the filter of our experiences. Don't hear what I'm not saying. We were given minds to think and thinking is not bad. The purpose of thinking is to process thoughts in order to come to conclusions and make decisions. Isaiah 55:8-9 reminds us, *"'For My thoughts are not your thoughts, neither are your ways My ways,' declares the LORD. 'As the heavens are higher than the earth, so are My ways higher than your ways and My thoughts than your thoughts."* His thoughts and ways are higher than ours which means that without Holy Spirit bringing us revelation as our Teacher, Counselor, and Guide, we cannot actually understand the ways of God. His thoughts and ways don't fit into this world; they are Heavenly. Listening is a form of receiving where the listener opens himself or herself to hear what the speaker is communicating without any preconceived notions. Therefore, it is important that we spend time listening for what He is saying in order to hear beyond our experience and understanding.

Many Ways to Hear

Over the years I've learned that the reason many people who claim that they don't hear from God is because they literally don't hear anything from God. However, they may feel, sense, know, or see things from God all the time, but they believe they don't hear from God because they literally don't hear. God also speaks through His Word and Holy Spirit will quicken or highlight words or portions of scripture. If you're one who believes you can't hear God's voice, I break that lie right now in the name of Jesus. I release the truth that you are one of His sheep and His sheep know His voice (John 10:4 NIV). Everyone hears from God, it's just whether we believe it or not! I give you permission to hear from God the way He speaks to YOU!

When we give ourselves permission to hear in our own unique way(s), we will accelerate the growth in our relationship with Him. When you meet a person for the first time you don't know their likes, dislikes, or preferences. You are not familiar with their usage of words, tone, or body language. All of these components of communication are an integral part of truly knowing someone. Wouldn't it be hard to get to know a friend if you weren't quite sure you were hearing what they were saying? Of course! It's the same in our relationship with Father God, Jesus, and Holy Spirit. Learn how God speaks to you and become a really good listener when you spend time with Him. I promise it will change your life!

Ask Questions

Questions are probably the greatest tool for relationship. Asking a question shows interest, looks for clarification, and seeks understanding. Asking questions invites dialogue and builds relationship. Asking questions admits you don't know all the answers and that you want to engage with the person you are communicating with.

Asking questions has led to more revelation than any other thing I've done to get to know God. Asking Him questions allows me to get to know His character, His ways, and His heart. I learned how to ask questions from my big brother, Jesus ☺ All throughout the Gospels, Jesus uses questions to get to the know our character, ways, and hearts. If Jesus' life is a model for how we are to live, then why not use the same principles of relationship with Him?

Give yourself permission to ask Him questions; all types of questions. Don't be afraid to ask the hard questions! I remember asking Him one specific question for several years. He always listened, but displayed wisdom by answering my hard question at the perfect time. God is good and He wants to you to "taste and see" that He is good (Psalm 34:8 NIV). Ask!

Not Hearing Anything?

As you go through the encounters in this section you may get to a point where you actually don't hear anything. That's ok. Let me repeat that...It's ok if you don't hear something! Many times, when I run into this in my times with the Lord, I will ask someone else. For example, when I take communion, I will ask Jesus, "What does this mean today?" If I don't hear (see, feel, sense, etc.) Jesus speaking to me, I will ask the same question again, but to Father God or Holy Spirit. If I ask Father God and I don't hear anything again, I will ask Holy Spirit. When I ask another person of the Godhead I hear something 99.999% of the time. The other 0.001% of the time, like the question it took Him several years to answer, His answer is His presence. No words, just His presence.

Pace Yourself

Each of these encounter activations is designed to help you step into freedom. If you are stepping into freedom, then that means you are stepping out of bondage. We all have it. We all need Jesus. I wouldn't recommend powering through this portion of the book. My recommendation would be to only complete one encounter activation per sitting. Why? When we get set free, our beliefs and perspectives shift spiritually and emotionally which can affect us physically. I've often felt "wiped" after experiencing a freedom encounter. I'm not saying you will. I'm just suggesting you pace yourself.

Staying Free

Many Christians will say "higher levels higher devils" and that is exactly what they often experience because of the truth of Proverbs 18:21, *"The tongue has the power of life and death, and those who love it will eat its fruit."* It is important to continue to agree with truth once you have encountered it. Declarations are a great tool for continuing to renew your mind and build your faith (in the new revelation of truth you have received during your encounter). Romans 10:17 (NKJV) reminds us that *"faith comes by hearing"*. Build your faith muscle by declaring the truths in the revelation you receive.

YOUR INVITATION

You are not reading this by accident. This is a divine appointment, right now, in this moment that you are reading this sentence. I believe the "more" you've been seeking will be unlocked as you journey through the next section of this book. I don't say this from a place of arrogance, but from a place of confidence, knowing that you will be set free in ways you've never before experienced because that's what happened to me when the Lord led me to them and through them.

Are you ready to for more freedom in your life? If so, I encourage you to approach each encounter with eyes to see, ears to hear, and a heart that is open. Jesus died on the cross so we could be free....so that you could be free.

Thank you for going on this journey with me. May you experience freedom beyond all that you've asked or imagined...

CHAPTER 7
WALKING THROUGH WALLS

ENCOUNTER TESTIMONY

One evening I was leading a woman through an encounter with Jesus. At one point, she saw herself walking on a pathway and at one point she came to a wall. The wall was black and tall. I asked her to look at the wall and see if she could see a word written on the wall. When she looked she saw the word "fear" written on the wall. I asked her if she was ready to take down the wall. She said she was. Then I had her ask Jesus to show her how to take down the wall. Jesus showed her that the wall was translucent and a mirage. She took Jesus' hand and took a step – through the wall! When she turned around to look for the wall it was gone! She asked Jesus what He wanted to give her to replace the wall and He gave her unconditional love!

INSTRUCTIONS

It's your turn for breakthrough and freedom from any walls that may be between you and Father God, Jesus, and Holy Spirit. Know that you may see more than one wall or you may not see any at all as you go on this encounter journey with the Godhead.

JESUS

Ask Jesus to show you a picture of any walls between you and Him.

What do you see?

_____

_____

_____

_____

_____

_____

_____

Ask Jesus to show you the word written on the wall.

What do you see?

_____
_____
_____
_____
_____
_____
_____
_____
_____
_____
_____
_____

Ask Jesus to show you how to tear down the wall.

What did He show you?

_____
_____
_____
_____
_____
_____
_____
_____
_____
_____
_____
_____
_____

Tear down the wall with Jesus. Then ask Jesus what truth He wants to give you in return.

What truth did He give you?

_____

_____

_____

_____

_____

_____

_____

_____

_____

_____

_____

_____

_____

HOLY SPIRIT
Ask Holy Spirit to show you a picture of any walls between you and Him.

What do you see?

_____

_____

_____

_____

_____

_____

_____

_____

Ask Holy Spirit to show you the word written on the wall.

What do you see?

_____
_____
_____
_____
_____
_____
_____
_____
_____
_____
_____
_____

Ask Holy Spirit to show you how to tear down the wall.

What did He show you?

_____
_____
_____
_____
_____
_____
_____
_____
_____
_____
_____
_____
_____

Tear down the wall with Holy Spirit. Then ask Holy Spirit what truth He wants to give you in return.

What truth did He give you?

_____
_____
_____
_____
_____
_____
_____
_____
_____

FATHER GOD

Ask Father God to show you a picture of any walls between you and Him.

What do you see?

_____
_____
_____
_____
_____
_____
_____
_____
_____
_____
_____
_____
_____

Ask Father God to show you the word written on the wall.

What do you see?

_____

_____

_____

_____

_____

_____

_____

_____

_____

_____

_____

_____

Ask Father God to show you how to tear down the wall.

What did He show you?

_____

_____

_____

_____

_____

_____

_____

_____

_____

_____

_____

_____

_____

Tear down the wall with Father God. Then ask Father God what truth He wants to give you in return.

What truth did He give you?

_____
_____
_____
_____
_____
_____
_____
_____
_____
_____
_____

Takeaways from this Activation:

_____
_____
_____
_____
_____
_____
_____
_____
_____
_____
_____
_____
_____
_____
_____
_____
_____

CHAPTER 8
ARROWS

ENCOUNTER TESTIMONY

We were doing a healing activation during the Activate course that I help lead. The facilitator had asked anyone with pain in their body to stand. Two people at my table stood up, Bob & Annabelle. Bob had pain in his lower back and Annabelle had pain in her mid-back. Chris, another guy at our table, was right next to Bob, and laid hands on him and commanded the pain to leave. We asked if he felt any shift in the pain level and Bob said no. We commanded the pain to leave again, and again no change. While the table kept praying, I asked Holy Spirit what was going on. Why wasn't the pain leaving? I immediately saw a picture in my mind's eye of arrows sticking out of Bob's back. I turned to Tim and motioned for him to imitate the motion of pulling something out of Bob's back. I didn't explain what Holy Spirit showed me, I just instructed him what to do. As soon as Tim did that motion (also known as a prophetic act) we all felt a shift in the atmosphere and Bob exclaimed that the pain was half of what it had been. Tim did the motion on the other side of Bob's back and ALL the pain left! Thank you, Jesus!

I explained to the table what Holy Spirit had showed me and when I finished, Annabelle immediately turned around and asked the person next to her to "pull out" the clump of arrows she saw in the middle of her back. When they did, her back was completely healed, too! Thank you, Jesus! When they shared what was happening with the entire class many of the students were freed from arrows that day!

INSTRUCTIONS

It's time to remove any arrows that may have been shot at you. As you go through asking each person of the Godhead to reveal any arrows remember that arrows are shot at you, not self-inflicted. You may not see any in one instance and you may see multiple in another. Remember to use your imagination to see what is being revealed and be encouraged because you are being set free!

JESUS
Ask Jesus to show you any arrows you may have.

What do you see?

_____

_____

_____

_____

_____

_____

_____

_____

_____

As a prophetic act, grab the arrow(s) with Jesus and pull them out.

What happened when you pulled the arrows out?

_____

_____

_____

_____

_____

_____

_____

_____

_____

_____

_____

Ask Jesus what truth He wants to fill the empty space with.

What did He show you?

_____
_____
_____
_____
_____
_____
_____
_____
_____
_____

HOLY SPIRIT
Ask Holy Spirit to show you any arrows you may have.

What do you see?

_____
_____
_____
_____
_____
_____
_____
_____
_____
_____
_____
_____
_____

As a prophetic act, grab the arrow(s) with Holy Spirit and pull them out.

What happened when you pulled the arrows out?

_____

_____

_____

_____

_____

_____

_____

_____

_____

Ask Holy Spirit what truth He wants to give you in return.

What did He show you?

_____

_____

_____

_____

_____

_____

_____

_____

_____

_____

_____

_____

_____

_____

_____

FATHER GOD
Ask Father God to show you any arrows you may have.

What do you see?

_____
_____
_____
_____
_____
_____
_____
_____
_____
_____
_____
_____
_____

As a prophetic act, grab the arrow(s) with Father God and pull them out.

What happened when you pulled the arrows out?

_____
_____
_____
_____
_____
_____
_____
_____
_____
_____
_____
_____
_____

Ask Father God what truth He wants to fill the empty space with.

What did He show you?

_____

_____

_____

_____

_____

_____

_____

_____

_____

_____

_____

_____

_____

Takeaways from this Activation:

_____

_____

_____

_____

_____

_____

_____

_____

_____

_____

_____

_____

_____

CHAPTER 9
REMOVING THE TAPE

ENCOUNTER TESTIMONY

A friend called to let me know she was wasn't feeling well and wasn't going to make it to a meeting she was helping lead that evening. She said she was really congested, and her throat was on fire. I asked if I could pray for her and Holy Spirit immediately reminded me of an encounter I had at a women's retreat. I was in a skit at a women's retreat where I played a woman who felt rejected. I spent the majority of the skit wearing a piece of masking tape with the word "REJECTED" scribbled in black permanent marker on it. When Holy Spirit brought that memory to mind I knew He wanted me to partner with Him to see if there was any tape on my friend. Using my imagination, I asked Holy Spirit to show me any labels on my friend. Holy Spirit showed me a piece of tape with the word "ANXIETY" on it. I shared it with my friend and told her to prophetically rip the tape off. She did and was able to breathe more freely. I asked Holy Spirit to show me anything else and I saw another piece of tape that had been under the first piece that said, "REJECTION." She ripped the tape off and felt overwhelming peace. I sensed that Holy Spirit had revealed all that was to be revealed. Talking to my friend later, she confirmed that both of those labels were things that had held her back in the past, and that she was able to not feel guilt or shame for missing the meeting for the first time!

INSTRUCTIONS

It's time to remove any labels you may be wearing. You may have put the tape on yourself or someone else may have put it on you – it doesn't matter. Remember, it's ok if you see no tape or multiple pieces of tape. This is part of your journey into more freedom!

JESUS
Ask Jesus to show you any tape you may be wearing.
What do you see?

_____

_____

_____

_____

_____

_____

_____

_____

_____

_____

_____

_____

_____

Ask Jesus to show you the word written on the tape.

What do you see?

_____

_____

_____

_____

_____

_____

_____

_____

_____

_____

_____

_____

As a prophetic act, grab the tape with Jesus and pull it off.

What happened when you pulled the tape off?

_____

_____

_____

_____

_____

_____

_____

_____

_____

_____

_____

Ask Jesus what truth He wants to give you in return.

What did He show you?

_____

_____

_____

_____

_____

_____

_____

_____

_____

_____

_____

_____

_____

HOLY SPIRIT
Ask Holy Spirit to show you any tape you may be wearing.

What do you see?

_____
_____
_____
_____
_____
_____
_____
_____
_____
_____
_____
_____

Ask Holy Spirit to show you the word written on the tape.

What do you see?

_____
_____
_____
_____
_____
_____
_____
_____
_____
_____
_____
_____

As a prophetic act, grab the tape with Holy Spirit and pull it off.

What happened when you pulled the tape off?

_____

_____

_____

_____

_____

_____

_____

_____

_____

_____

_____

_____

Ask Holy Spirit what truth He wants to give you in return.

What did He show you?

_____

_____

_____

_____

_____

_____

_____

_____

_____

_____

_____

_____

FATHER GOD

Ask Father God to show you any tape you may be wearing.

What do you see?

_____

_____

_____

_____

_____

_____

_____

_____

_____

_____

_____

Ask Father God to show you the word written on the tape.

What do you see?

_____

_____

_____

_____

_____

_____

_____

_____

_____

_____

_____

As a prophetic act, grab the tape with Father God and pull it off.

What happened when you pulled the tape off?

_____

_____

_____

_____

_____

_____

_____

_____

_____

_____

_____

_____

Ask Father God what truth He wants to give you in return.

What did He show you?

_____

_____

_____

_____

_____

_____

_____

_____

_____

_____

_____

_____

Takeaways from this Activation:

_____

_____

_____

_____

_____

_____

_____

_____

_____

_____

_____

_____

_____

_____

_____

_____

_____

_____

_____

_____

_____

_____

_____

_____

_____

_____

_____

_____

_____

_____

_____

_____

_____

CHAPTER 10
CHECK YOUR HEART

ENCOUNTER TESTIMONY

My friend and I were praying for another friend one night after a training we had at church. I always begin praying for someone by asking Holy Spirit what He wants to say to them. When I did this, I was reminded of an encounter that I had where Jesus showed me my heart. I've partnered with Holy Spirit long enough to know that when something comes to mind that He's saying He wants to do it again for whomever I'm praying for. I asked my friend to ask Holy Spirit to show her a picture of her heart. She immediately saw a picture of a cartoon heart that was cinched in the middle by a metal clamp. I instructed her to ask Holy Spirit to show her if there was a word on the clamp. When she asked, she saw the word "long-suffering". Then I told her to ask Holy Spirit to remove the clamp of long suffering from her heart. In the picture Holy Spirit was showing her, she saw the metal clamp pop off, and the cartoon heart that represented her heart bounced out, one side and then the other. Then I told her to ask Holy Spirit what He wanted to give her in return. She then saw a gold ribbon encircle her heart and tie itself in a bow. I asked her to see if she could see a word on the golden bow that had just been tied around her heart. When she looked she saw the word "love". My friend shared a prophetic word that Holy Spirit was showing her. As we finished, all three of us could feel the shift that had happened in the atmosphere.

The next day, the friend that we had prayed for shared that Holy Spirit had given her even more revelation about the long-suffering that had been a clamp around her heart. First, He led her through forgiving people that she felt had caused long-suffering in her life. Then Holy Spirit revealed some bitterness in her heart, blaming God Himself for the long-suffering she had experienced. In His goodness, He revealed it, and invited her into forgiving Him too.

INSTRUCTIONS

In Psalm 139:23 (NIV) David invites the Lord, "*Search me, God, and know my heart; test me and know my anxious thoughts.*" David was inviting the Lord to help him do a heart check. This is an opportunity to invite the Lord to do a heart check with you. Remember to stay open to seeing whatever He wants to show you. He's a good, good Father and is Love. He wants to love you through this encounter so that you can be whole and free!

GIVE THE INVITATION
Ask Holy Spirit to show you a picture of your heart.

What did He show you?

_____
_____
_____
_____
_____
_____
_____
_____
_____
_____

Ask Holy Spirit if there are any words attached to what you see.

What did He show you?

_____
_____
_____
_____
_____
_____
_____
_____

Ask Holy Spirit to remove anything restricting or negative that He reveals.

What happened?

_____
_____
_____
_____
_____
_____
_____
_____
_____
_____
_____
_____

Ask Holy Spirit what He would like to give you in place of what was removed.

What did Holy Spirit give you instead?

_____
_____
_____
_____
_____
_____
_____
_____
_____
_____
_____

Takeaways from this Activation:

CHAPTER 11
FEASTING IN HIS PRESENCE

ENCOUNTER TESTIMONY

I was visiting friends at Bethel Church, Redding for a few days and had the opportunity to attend the healing rooms. The healing room experience begins with a short introduction and teaching that explains healing. The experience continues in the Encounter Room where individuals wait their turn for prayer. The Encounter Room is filled with all types of worship. There was a team leading worship from the stage, artists painting, worship dancers dancing, and teams of people walking around the room, praying. There were clusters of chairs throughout the room where we could sit if we wanted. I sat down and a few minutes later two of the worship dancers came over and asked if they could pray for me. I agreed and they began giving me a prophetic word. Part of the prophetic word was Psalm 23:5 (NIV), *"You prepare a table before me in the presence of my enemies."* This verse brought confirmation to a situation I was experiencing, and I was encouraged that I could prosper regardless of whatever situation or circumstance I experience!

INSTRUCTIONS

Gather some paper, a bible, and communion elements. On each piece of paper write down an "enemy" that you feel like you've been facing; a person, situation, or circumstance. Make sure to only write one "enemy" per piece of paper. Then lay out the pieces of paper in front of you or around you. Take your bible in your hands and ponder the truth that you are holding the sword of the spirit (Ephesians 6:17 NIV). In front of all the "enemies" spend a few minutes "feasting" on the Word of God. Ask Holy Spirit to lead you. When you are done feasting on the Word enjoy the next course of your feast as you take communion. Ask Jesus what He wants to reveal to you through communion in this moment. Reflect on your experience after the encounter.

What enemies have you been facing?

_____
_____
_____
_____
_____
_____
_____
_____
_____
_____
_____
_____

Describe what you experienced while feasting on the Word of
God in the presence of your "enemies." What did you see, feel,
hear, etc.?

_____
_____
_____
_____
_____
_____
_____
_____
_____
_____
_____
_____
_____
_____

What revelations(s) did you receive feasting on the Word?

_____
_____
_____
_____
_____
_____
_____
_____
_____
_____
_____
_____
_____
_____

Describe your experience taking communion in the presence of your "enemies." What did you see, feel, hear, etc.?

_____
_____
_____
_____
_____
_____
_____
_____
_____
_____
_____
_____
_____

What revelations(s) did you receive while taking communion?

_____

_____

_____

_____

_____

_____

_____

_____

_____

_____

_____

_____

_____

_____

How do you feel about your "enemies" after this encounter?

_____

_____

_____

_____

_____

_____

_____

_____

_____

_____

_____

_____

_____

_____

_____

Takeaways from this Activation:

_____
_____
_____
_____
_____
_____
_____
_____
_____
_____
_____
_____
_____
_____
_____
_____
_____
_____
_____
_____
_____
_____
_____
_____
_____
_____
_____
_____
_____
_____
_____
_____
_____
_____
_____
_____

CHAPTER 12
KNOW YOUR NAME

ENCOUNTER TESTIMONY

The meaning of names is important. Names give identity and when a name is spoken that identity is released over you. Isaac's name meant laugher (Genesis 21:1-6 NIV). Gomer made statements through the names of her children. Her daughter was named Lo-Ruhamah which means "not loved" and a son named Lo-Ammi which means "not my people" (Hosea 1:6-9 NIV). Peter's name meant "rock" and Jesus declared *you are Peter, and on this rock I will build my church*" (Matthew 16:18 NIV).

My name, Sarah, means Princess. The Lord used the meaning of my name to reveal revelations of His love for me through several Valentine's Day encounters. I'm not going to take time here to share those stories again, but you can read them in my first book, Encounter Jesus. I've also received numerous prophetic words over the years from people that don't even know my name. Every time someone calls me Sarah they are declaring my identity over me. Every time I am called by name, royalty, beauty, and authority are being released over me. It's a game changer!

INSTRUCTIONS

Google what your name means. Scroll through the results and see what Holy Spirit highlights to you. What He highlights may not be from a "Christian" website and that's ok. What is important is that you partner with Holy Spirit to see what He is saying. For example, Holy Spirit used the Kung Fu Panda movies to share several revelations about identity with me. He wasn't endorsing another religion, He was using something in the natural, in this case a movie, to speak His truth to me.

Romans 8:1 (NIV) says, *"Therefore, there is now no condemnation for those who are in Christ Jesus."* If you discover your name means something negative, filter it through this truth and declare the opposite. I remember looking up someone's name and found that the meaning of their name was "darkness" so I declared that they were "light" instead. The Lord always speaks words over us that are "full of Spirit and life" (John 6:63 NIV).

What does your name mean?

_____
_____
_____
_____
_____
_____
_____
_____
_____
_____
_____
_____

What was your initial reaction to the meaning of your name? Why?

_____
_____
_____
_____
_____
_____
_____
_____
_____
_____
_____

Are there times where you have experienced the opposite of the life-giving definition of your name? If so, explain.

_____

_____

_____

_____

_____

_____

_____

_____

_____

_____

_____

_____

_____

What are some ways the meaning of your name can influence your identity?

_____

_____

_____

_____

_____

_____

_____

_____

_____

_____

_____

_____

_____

Takeaways from this Activation:

_____
_____
_____
_____
_____
_____
_____
_____
_____
_____
_____
_____
_____
_____
_____
_____
_____
_____
_____
_____
_____
_____
_____
_____
_____
_____
_____
_____
_____
_____
_____
_____
_____
_____
_____
_____
_____

CHAPTER 13
COME HOLY SPIRIT

ENCOUNTER TESTIMONY

My church was hosting a children's conference and I was on the ministry team that night. They released us in pairs throughout the sanctuary to minister to people. My team got to a group of young men and we began to prophesy over each of them. As my team member prayed, the Holy Spirit reminded me of Jesus' baptism (Luke 3:21-22 NIV) and prompted me to ask the young man if he had ever invited the Dove to come and remain on him. He had not so I asked the young man if he would like to now. He agreed and repeated after me, "Holy Spirit, I invite you to come, descend on me like a dove, and remain." I asked if he sensed anything and he reported that he was feeling heat all over his body. Holy Spirit had come, and he was encountering the presence of God in a new way!

INSTRUCTIONS

Get in a quiet space when you have a few minutes. Out loud, invite Holy Spirit to come and remain. Allow yourself to "marinate" in the moment, tuning into anything you may be feeling, seeing, imagining, knowing, or hearing. Allow Holy Spirit to come and keep coming. Take time to reflect on this encounter.

In what ways did you experience Holy Spirit in ways you haven't before?

_____
_____
_____
_____
_____
_____
_____
_____
_____

What revelation did you receive from this encounter with the Holy Spirit?

_____
_____
_____
_____
_____
_____
_____
_____
_____
_____
_____
_____

Imagine Holy Spirit sitting on your shoulder in the form of a Dove. Ask Him to share a secret with you.

What did Holy Spirit share with you?

_____
_____
_____
_____
_____
_____
_____
_____
_____
_____
_____
_____

Continue to imagine Holy Spirit as the Dove sitting on your shoulder. Ask Him to encourage you.

How did Holy Spirit encourage you?

_____

_____

_____

_____

_____

_____

_____

_____

_____

_____

_____

_____

Takeaways from this Activation:

_____

_____

_____

_____

_____

_____

_____

_____

_____

_____

_____

_____

_____

CHAPTER 14
WHAT DO YOU CARRY?

ENCOUNTER TESTIMONY

I was attending a conference, and during worship a few days into the conference, I had an encounter with an angel. I was standing there singing with my eyes closed. Often times during worship I will partner with Holy Spirit and use my imagination to tune in to "see" what is happening in the room. This particular day I knew, and then saw, an angel standing in front of me. I had recently heard someone share that when you see an angel you should ask them their name and their assignment. I honestly don't remember what the angel's name was. When I asked what the angel's assignment was, I was handed a small vase in my right hand and another small vase in my left hand. The angel went on to share that in my right hand, it was a small vase filled with peace, and in my left hand it was a small vase of joy. I had never had an encounter like this before nor seen an angel, so it was easy to believe and receive by faith.

A few months later, I was on my way to a meeting with one of my students. We got on an elevator and I could tell she immediately began to feel anxious. I asked her what was wrong, and she said that she was claustrophobic. Without saying a word, I intentionally put my right hand, the one with peace, on her shoulder and told her it would be ok. Her eyes got big and she looked at me and asked, "What are you doing?" I asked her what she meant, and she said that as soon as I put my hand on her shoulder that she felt a calm come over her and the anxiety leave. By faith, I was releasing the peace that I had received during my encounter. What does Holy Spirit want to give you to carry and release to the world?

INSTRUCTIONS

Hold out your hands in front of you as a prophetic act that you are about to receive something. Close your eyes and imagine Jesus standing in front of you. In your imagination, watch Him place an object in your right hand. Once you see the object ask Him what it represents. Now watch as Jesus puts another object in your left hand. Once you see the object ask Him what it represents. Record and reflect on this encounter.

What did Jesus put in your right hand?

_____
_____
_____
_____
_____
_____
_____
_____
_____
_____
_____
_____
_____

What did Jesus say the object represented?

_____
_____
_____
_____
_____
_____
_____
_____
_____
_____
_____
_____
_____

What did Jesus put in your left hand?

_____
_____
_____
_____
_____
_____
_____
_____
_____
_____
_____
_____

What did Jesus say the object represented?

_____
_____
_____
_____
_____
_____
_____
_____
_____
_____
_____
_____

List several ways you could practice releasing the new revelation of what you carry:

_____
_____
_____
_____
_____

Takeaways from this Activation:

_____
_____
_____
_____
_____
_____
_____
_____
_____
_____
_____
_____
_____
_____
_____
_____
_____
_____
_____
_____
_____
_____
_____
_____
_____
_____
_____
_____
_____
_____
_____
_____
_____

CHAPTER 15
NEW NAME

ENCOUNTER TESTIMONY

The bible is full of encounters where names were given with specific intentions. Abram's name was changed to Abraham (Genesis 17:5 NIV). Sarai's name was changed to Sarah (Genesis 17:15 NIV). Jacob's name was changed to Israel (Genesis 32:28 NIV). Saul's name was changed to Paul (Acts 13:9 NIV). The angel of the Lord appeared to Gideon and called him "Mighty Warrior" (Judges 6:12 NIV). Names are important!

After graduating with my master's degree, I began working at a campus ministry at Florida State University. Part of my responsibilities included mentoring and discipling our students. One day in our staff meeting, my boss informed me that some of the students I had been meeting with had come to him complaining that I was "mean". I was completely caught off guard. Later that evening I was laying on my face before the Lord. I was explaining to Him that I didn't understand why the students felt that I was being mean. I began examining my heart to see if I had any mean motives or anger in my heart – nothing. My heart was fully towards them and for them. I felt misunderstood, hurt, and confused. In that moment the Lord spoke to me, and I heard Him say in that inner audible voice inside my head, "I call you Loving Kindness." I know it was the Lord because that is not something I would have come up with on my own or said about myself; especially in that moment. I like to think of this encounter as my Gideon moment where the Lord spoke identity and the opposite of what I was experiencing over me. Gideon was hiding, I was accused of being mean. The Lord called Gideon Mighty Warrior, and He called me Loving Kindness. These new names are the exact opposite of the current experience. What is the Lord's new name for you?

INSTRUCTIONS

Picture Jesus standing in front of you. Imagine him handing you a scroll. Untie the ribbon from the scroll, open it, and read the new name He has given you. Research the meaning of the name (Google it, look it up in the dictionary, etc.). Remember if what you see doesn't make sense, ask Jesus questions and listen for His answers. Take time to reflect on this encounter below.

What did you see written on the scroll?

_____
_____
_____
_____
_____
_____
_____
_____
_____
_____
_____
_____
_____
_____
_____

What was your initial reaction to the name He gave you?

_____
_____
_____
_____
_____
_____
_____
_____
_____
_____
_____

What does the name mean?

_____
_____
_____
_____
_____
_____
_____
_____
_____

How does this name speak to your identity?

_____
_____
_____
_____
_____
_____
_____
_____
_____
_____
_____
_____
_____

Takeaways from this Activation:

_____
_____
_____
_____
_____
_____
_____
_____
_____

CHAPTER 16
BE HEALED

ENCOUNTER TESTIMONY

I received a text one afternoon from one of our school of ministry students, saying that she had a migraine and was going to miss class that evening. Something rose up inside of me as I read her text, and I thought of the story in Acts 19 where people were getting healed and delivered as they came into contact with Paul's handkerchief. In that moment I decided to take a risk. I didn't have a handkerchief, but I did have a cell phone. If an object Paul touched could carry the anointing to heal and deliver, why couldn't another object? I texted the student back asking her to put her cell phone to her forehead and leave it there while I texted declarations of healing over her. I instructed her to wait until she stopped hearing the text notifications and then to reply letting me know if she noticed any shifts or changes. She agreed to try it and put the cell phone to her head while I texted, "Pain leave. By His stripes (Isaiah 53:5) you are healing. Headache go in Jesus' name". She replied back, saying that the pain in her head hadn't changed, but the nausea she had been feeling was completely gone. She put her phone on her head again and I texted more declarations. She replied back, saying she was feeling better, the pain in her head hadn't left yet, and that she just felt like she needed to sleep for an hour. She said she'd let me know how she was doing when she woke up. I headed to school to get ready for the evening, and instead of texting me back she showed up for class without any pain or nausea!

INSTRUCTIONS

I want to pray for any physical healing you may need in your body. Take the book, just like the handkerchief and cell phone, and place the declarations on the next page on whatever body part needs healing. Hold the declaration page on your body for 10 seconds and then check to see if you sense any shifts (pain level, mobility, breathing, etc.). Thank Jesus for any improvements you notice. Jesus died for 100% of your pain. Give yourself permission to pray more than once for the same body part. Repeat this process for any other parts of your body that need healing. Reflect on your encounter below.

Healing Declarations

Pain leave.

By His stripes I am healed.

Body function the way God created you to function.

Body you are healthy and whole.

What parts of your body needing healing and how high was the pain on a scale of 0 (no pain) to 10 (extreme pain) before you started?

_____

_____

_____

_____

_____

_____

_____

_____

_____

_____

What shifts did you sense or feel in your body (pain level, mobility, breathing, etc.)?

_____

_____

_____

_____

Who is someone you know that needs healing that you could pray for over text? Plan a time to pray for them.

_____
_____
_____
_____
_____
_____
_____
_____
_____
_____
_____
_____
_____

Takeaways from this Activation:

_____
_____
_____
_____
_____
_____
_____
_____
_____
_____
_____
_____
_____
_____

WHAT NOW?

Beloved,

Practice.
Take risks.
Leave your comfort zone.
Step out of the boat.
Try something.
Try something else.
Set aside time.
Do relationship.
Do relationship some more.

Father God created you.
Jesus died for you.
Holy Spirit lives within you.

They see you.
They know you.
They love you.
They want relationship with you.

End of story.

beENCOUNTERed,

Sarah

P.S. - I would love to hear and share testimonies of breakthrough, freedom, and healing you have experienced while reading this book.

Please email them to sarah@beencountered.com.

ADDITIONAL RESOURCES

VISIT
www.beencountered.com

BOOKS

Cultivating Awareness and Intimacy
A Practical Guide

ENCOUNTER
JESUS

SARAH CROCKETT

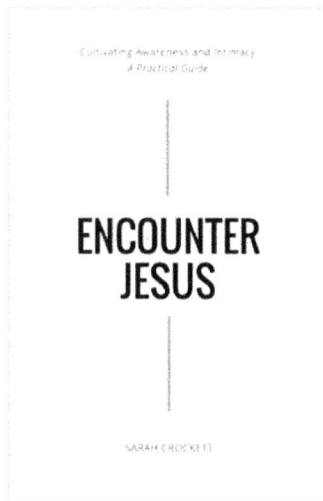

ENCOUNTER ACTIVATION SERIES

Five Practical Keys For Having Encounters With God

A Simple Tool For Hearing The Voice Of God

15 Questions For Strengthening Your Connection

E-COURSES

BREAKING FREE:
Overcoming Fear, Shame, & Insecurity

FREE – PROMO CODE: UNSTUCK

UNLOCKING THE POWER OF WORDS

WITH SARAH CROCKETT

ONLY $27

STAY CONNECTED

Facebook - @beENCOUNTERed
Instagram - @beENCOUNTERed

www.ingramcontent.com/pod-product-compliance
Lightning Source LLC
Chambersburg PA
CBHW071227090426
42736CB00014B/3001